Coding for Beginners Using PYTHON TURTLE

Textbook

5

Sangita Chadha

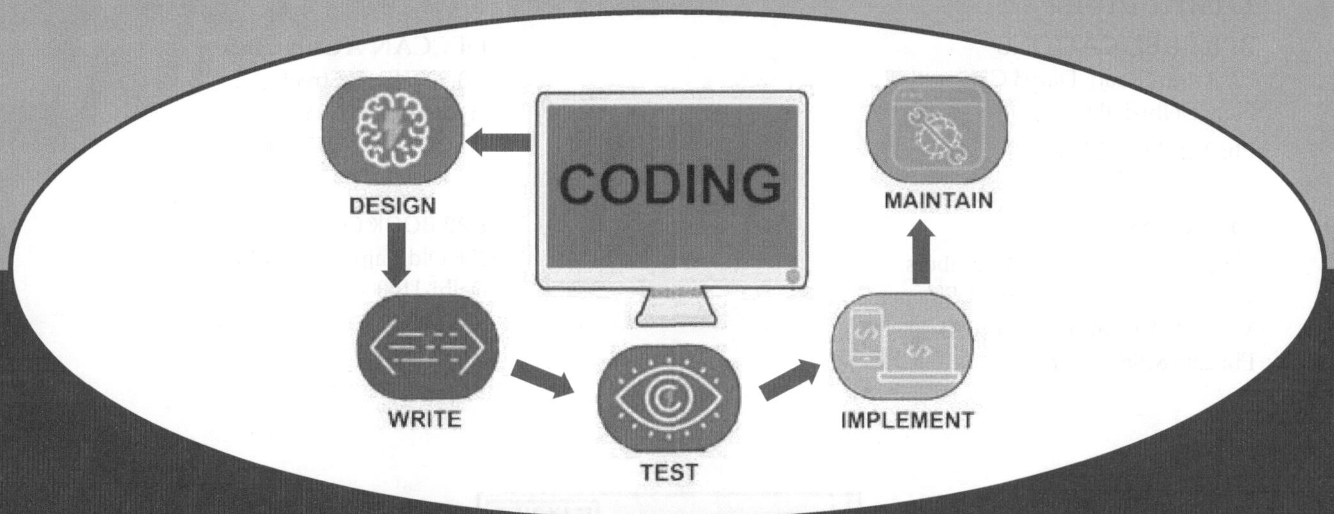

www.bpbonline.com

FIRST EDITION 2022
REPRINT 2025

ISBN: 978-93-5551-223-9

Distributors:

BPB PUBLICATIONS
20, Ansari Road, Darya Ganj
New Delhi-110002
Ph: 23254990/23254991

DECCAN AGENCIES
4-3-329, Bank Street,
Hyderabad-500195
Ph: 24756967/24756400

MICRO MEDIA
Shop No. 5, Mahendra Chambers,
150 DN Rd. Next to Capital Cinema,
V.T. (C.S.T.) Station, MUMBAI-400 001
Ph: 22078296/22078297

BPB BOOK CENTRE
376 Old Lajpat Rai Market,
Delhi-110006
Ph: 23861747

To View Complete BPB Publications Catalogue Scan the QR Code:

Published by Manish Jain for BPB Publications, 20 Ansari Road, Darya Ganj, New Delhi-110002 and Printed by him at Manipal Technologies Limited, Manip[al

www.bpbonline.com

Dedicated to

My children and students

About the Authors

Sangita Chadha has been working as Head of Computer Department in Ambience Public School, Safdarjung Enclave, New Delhi from last 14 years. She has over twenty years of experience in the field of education; teaching Computer Science, Informatics Practices and Multimedia & Web Technology to grades XI and XII; and has been multifold responsibilities at her school (Result In-charge, ERP, Website, Almanac, Magazine). She is a passionate learner and committed educator consistently working to make learning enjoyable for the learners.Her foremost classroom pedagogy is centered around project-based learning. She has conducted ICT and Net safety workshops for all stakeholders. She has been part of the curriculum development team for classes IX and X Information and Communication Technology, NCERT. She has co-authored class IX and X ICT for NCERT. She also co-authored Class XII Informatics Practices and Computer Science, NCERT. She has conducted Teacher Training workshops for SCERT Teachers.

Acknowledgements

I would like to acknowledge the contributions of all the educators, data scientists, scientists, professionals from various fields for their valuable suggestions in developing the content for this book.

I would like to express my gratitude to everyone at BPB Publications for giving us this opportunity to write the book. I am thankful to all the resource persons at BPB Publications for editing, technical reviewing and language editing the book. I would like to thank our technical reviewer, Mrs. Rekha Verma for her thoughtful insights while refining the manuscript of this book.

I am thankful to my family for being supportive in numerous ways and for giving their unconditional love and support at all times.

Lastly, but not the least, I would like to thank God for bearing us with courage and humility to be able to write this book for our students.

— Sangita Chadha

Preface

The primary objective in the development of this book series is to create a fun learning and project-based approach to start learning coding. With the help of this, the student will be able to understand, identify and apply the fundamentals of a programming language. It also builds problem-solving skills.

Book will bring an innovative approach among students by Project-based learning which fosters creativity, critical thinking, and innovative ideas that enable a deeper understanding of concepts which leads to longer retention. We make learning of complex concepts fun and focus on real-life applications.

The students will start with the approach of looking at the application first and then follow the steps to build an application. They will learn by doing as we all know that once we practice we remember it for our lifetime.

Contents

Installation Guide

Visual Studio Code can be used as an excellent editor for many languages with the help of extensions. It is simple, easy, fun, small in size, and productive. The extensions available make it an excellent editor and are operating system independent.

Students are required to go through the following links to download and install the Python interpreter and then download and install Visual Studio Code.

Follow the instructions while using the links given below as per your operating system to install Python and Visual Studio Code:

- Python on Linux:

  https://www.python.org/downloads/source/

- Visual Studio Code on Linux:

  https://code.visualstudio.com/docs/setup/linux

- Python on macOS:

  https://www.python.org/downloads/mac-osx/

- Visual Studio Code on macOS:

  https://code.visualstudio.com/docs/setup/mac

- Python on Windows:

  https://www.python.org/downloads/windows/

- Visual Studio Code on Windows:

  https://code.visualstudio.com/docs/setup/windows

- Check out the following links to know more about the Visual Studio code:

  https://code.visualstudio.com/docs

  https://code.visualstudio.com/docs/getstarted/tips-and-tricks

Introduction to Python, Turtle and Visual Studio Code

Introduction to Python

- Python is a most popular, high-level, and open-source programming language.
- It is a powerful, fast, interactive, object-oriented, and dynamic programming language.
- It is easy to learn and can run on any platform.
- It is a case-sensitive language. That means uppercase and lowercase letters are not treated the same.

Introduction to Turtle

- It is a module that is pre-installed with Python.
- Enables to draw shapes, images and any kind of designs on a canvas (drawing screen).
- The pen helps to draw on the canvas is known as turtle.
- Helps to create animations.
- Turtle can be used to create games.

Steps to use Visual Studio Code:

- **Open Visual Studio Code** – Click on the Windows key and type in Visual Studio Code. Click on Visual Studio Code to open the application.

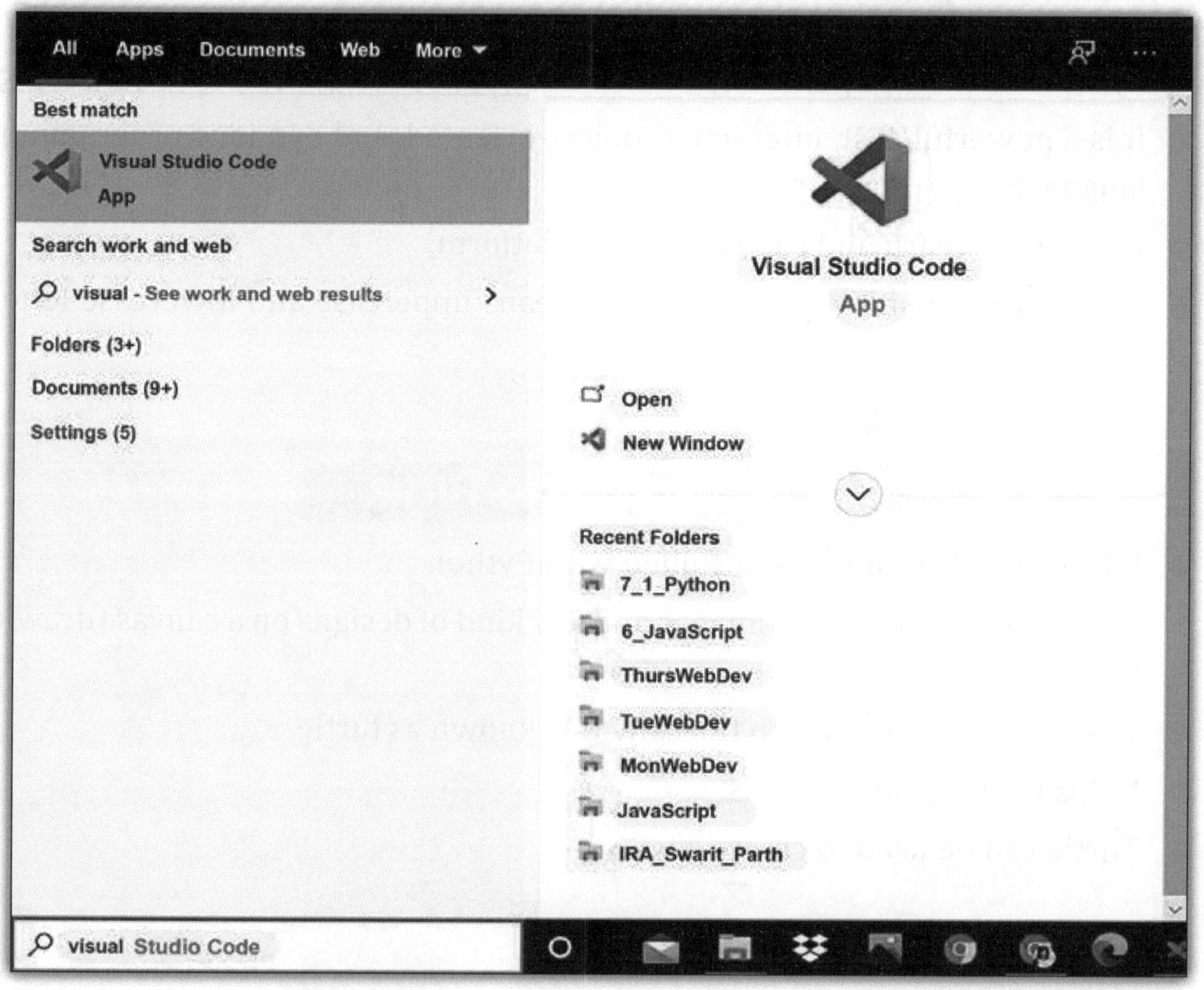

Figure 1.1: Opening of Visual Studio Code

- The Visual Studio Code application looks like as shown in figure 1.2.

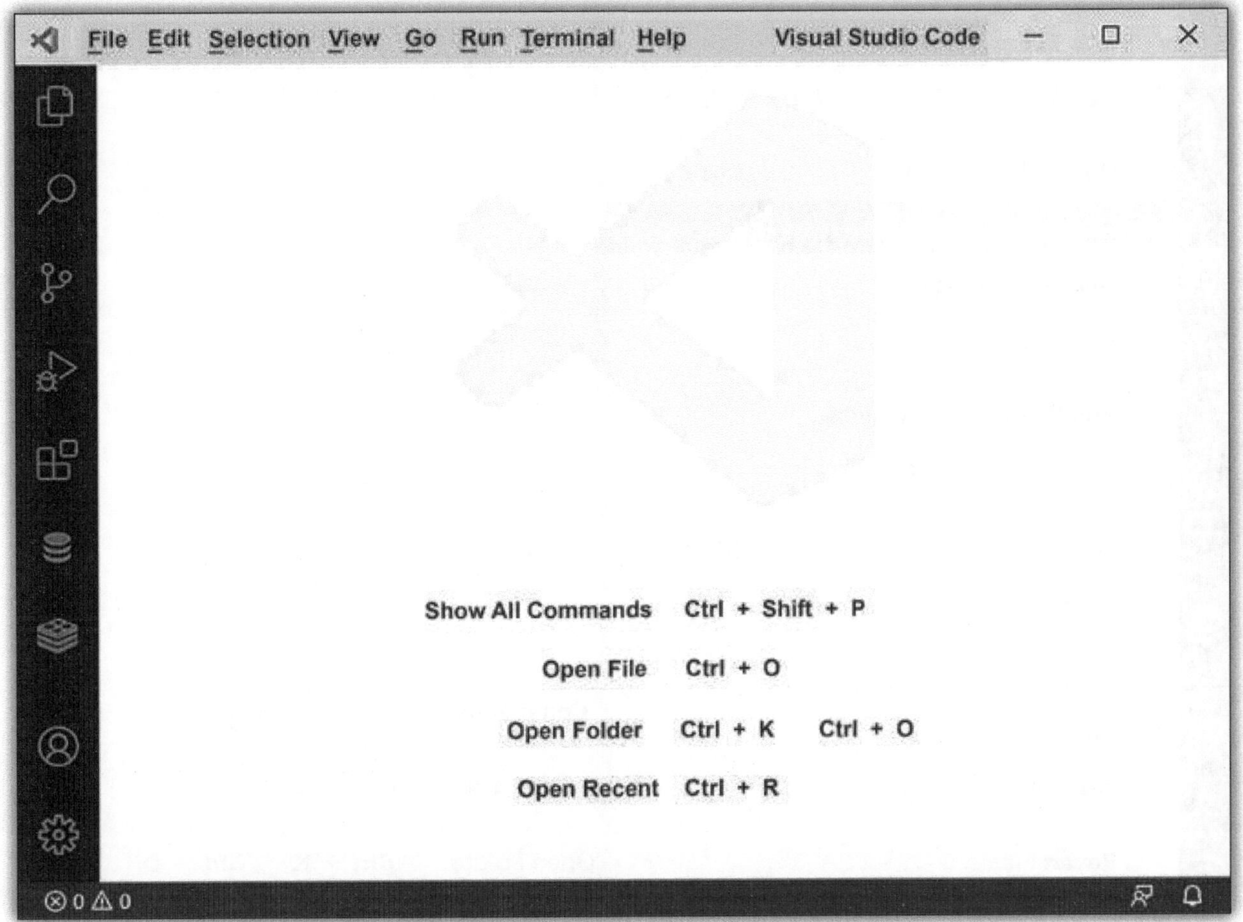

Figure 1.2: Visual Studio Code window

- Now, let us open the folder (i.e. the work area) to place all the python files in that folder. Click on File Open Folder as shown in figure 1.3(a) and then choose the folder to work with.

  For first-time users, a new folder needs to be created.

Choose the path, click on New Folder, and give a name to the folder as shown in figure 1.3 (b) (For first-time users). Then click on the folder name to choose it and click on Select Folder as shown in figure 1.3(c) will open the work area for your python files in Visual Studio Code.

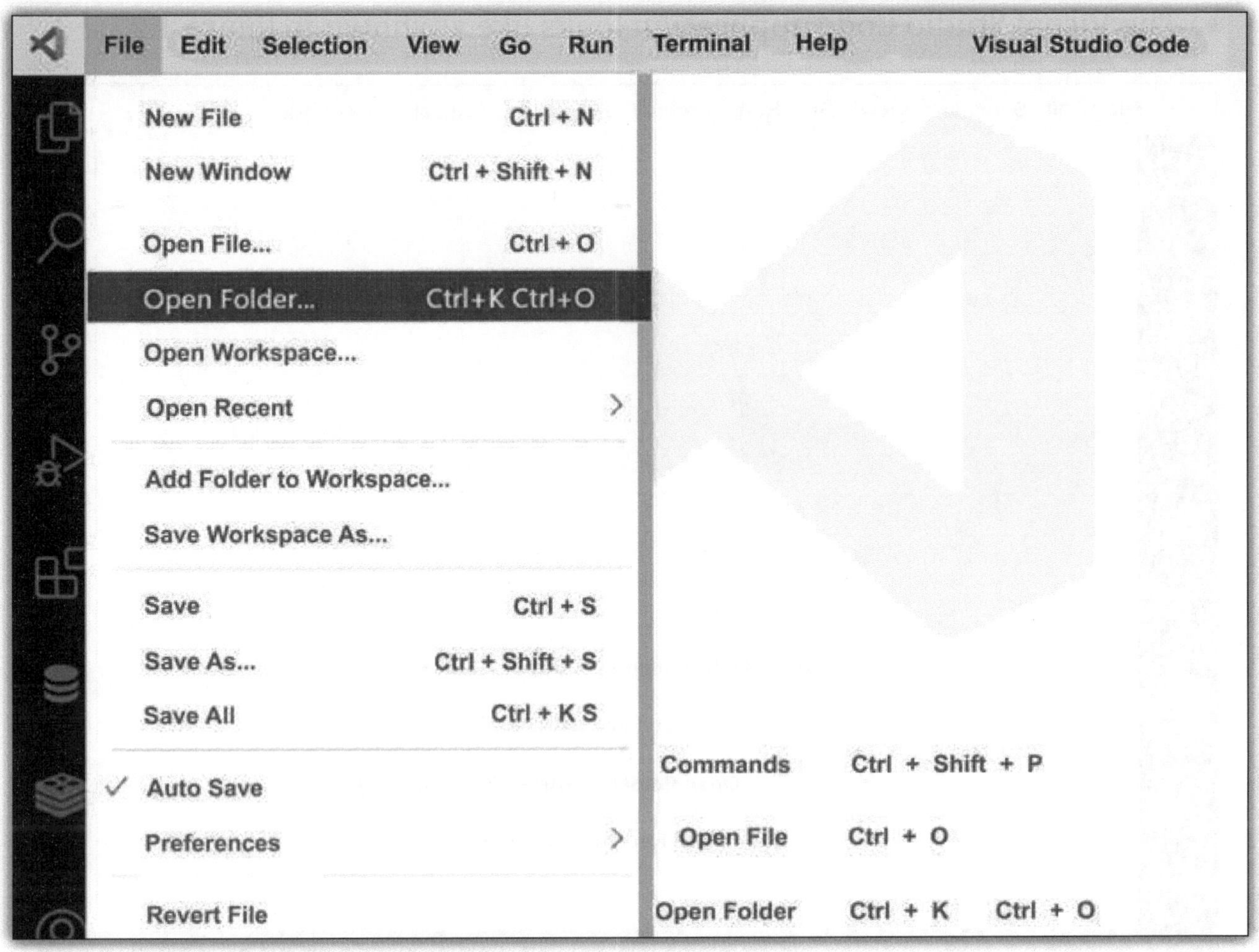

Figure 1.3(a): Open Folder

Choose the path, click on New Folder, and give a name to the folder as shown in figure 1.3 (b) (For first-time users). Then click on the folder name to choose it and click on Select Folder as shown in figure 1.3(c) will open the work area for your python files in Visual Studio Code.

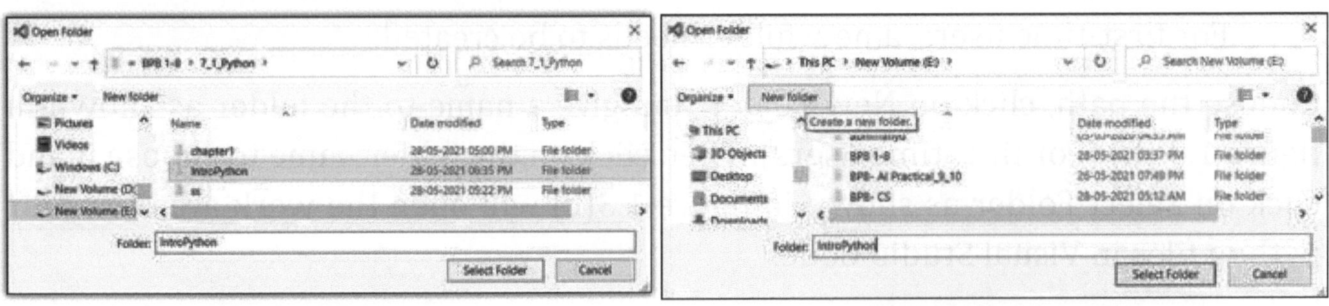

Figure 1.3(b)

Figure 1.3(c)

Write the filename and put the extension

.py

Click on this icon to create a new file

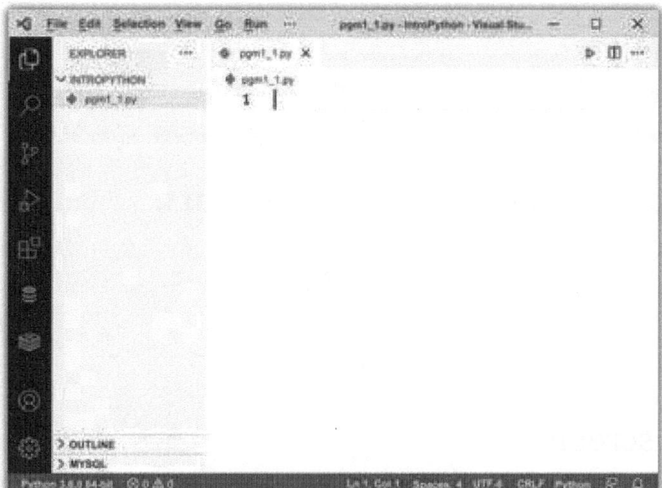

Figure 1.3(d)

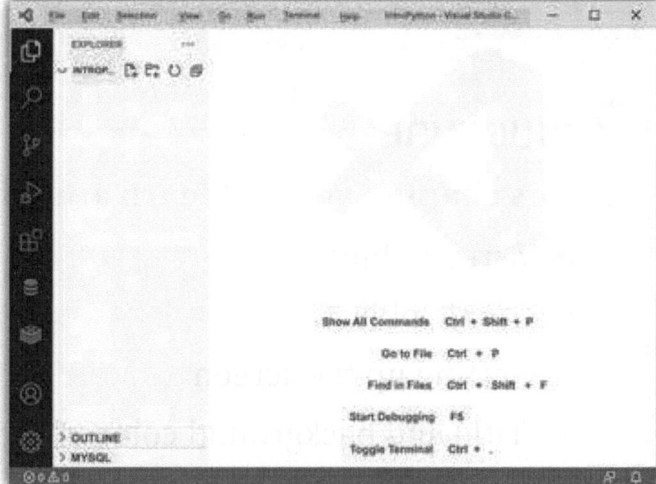

Figure 1.3(e)

Terminal Window to display the output of the code

Code Editor Window

Click on this icon to execute the code

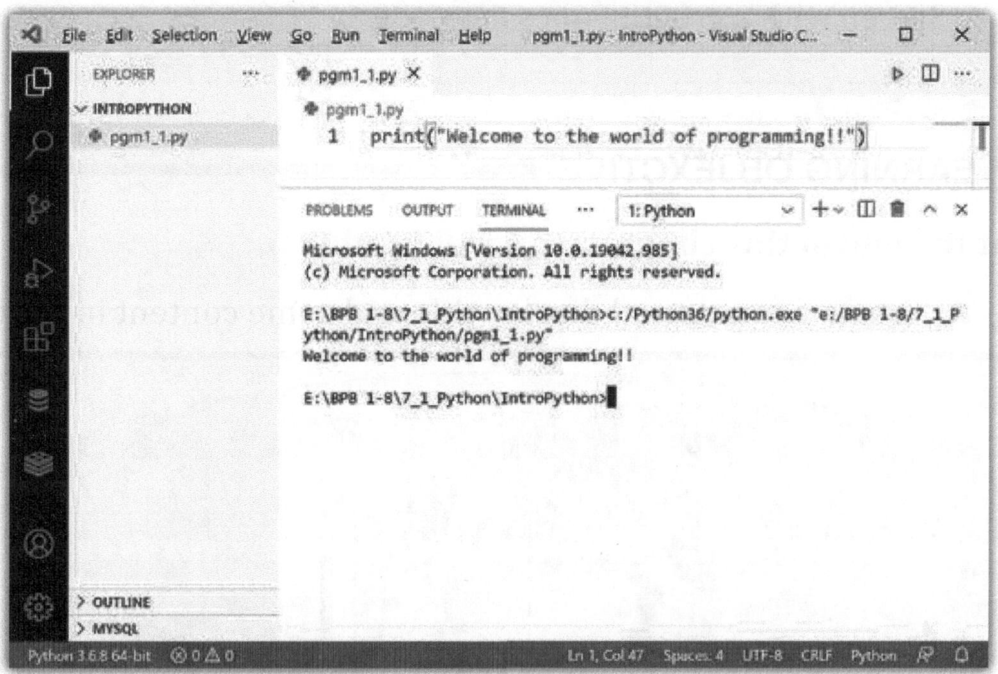

Figure 1.4: Visual Studio Code window

2 Playing with Color and Text

STRUCTURE

In this chapter, you will learn and practice the following concepts:

- Screen object
- Turtle object
- Setting up the screen
- Title and background color of the screen
- Writing text
- Changing the style, size, and color of the text

PROJECT

Screen with a greeting message

LEARNING OBJEXCTIVE

At the end of this chapter, you will be able to:

- Create a canvas and display title and some content in the canvas

Turtle is a pre-defined library/ module in Python that helps the users to create shapes, objects to showcase the creativity on a drawing board known as **canvas**. The pen with the help of which the user draws on canvas is called the **turtle**.

To use turtle module in Python, use the following command:

```
import turtle
```

To create an instance of the canvas/ screen so that turtle can work on it, use the following command:

```
scr = turtle.Screen()
```

The scr is an instance and you can use any name for the instance.

To setup the screen size of the canvas, use the following command:

```
scr.screensize(400, 300)
```

Here, 400 is the width of the canvas and 300 is its height.

To display the title on the title bar of the canvas, the following command can be used:

```
scr.title("My Canvas")
```

To change the background color of the canvas, the following command can be used:

```
scr.bgcolor('black')
```

Info Bot

Turtle can be placed to the desired location by understanding the coordinates in the turtle screen as shown in the figure 2.3.

Activity 2.1

Write the code to create a canvas with pink background color and title of the window 'My First Canvas' as shown in figure 2.1 (a).

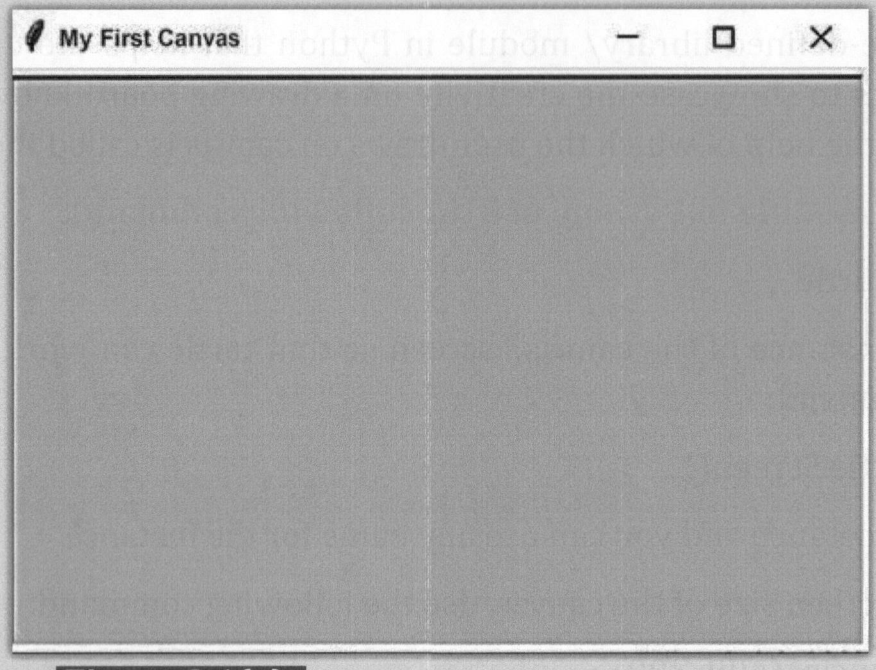

Figure 2.1(a): Output window for Activity 2.1

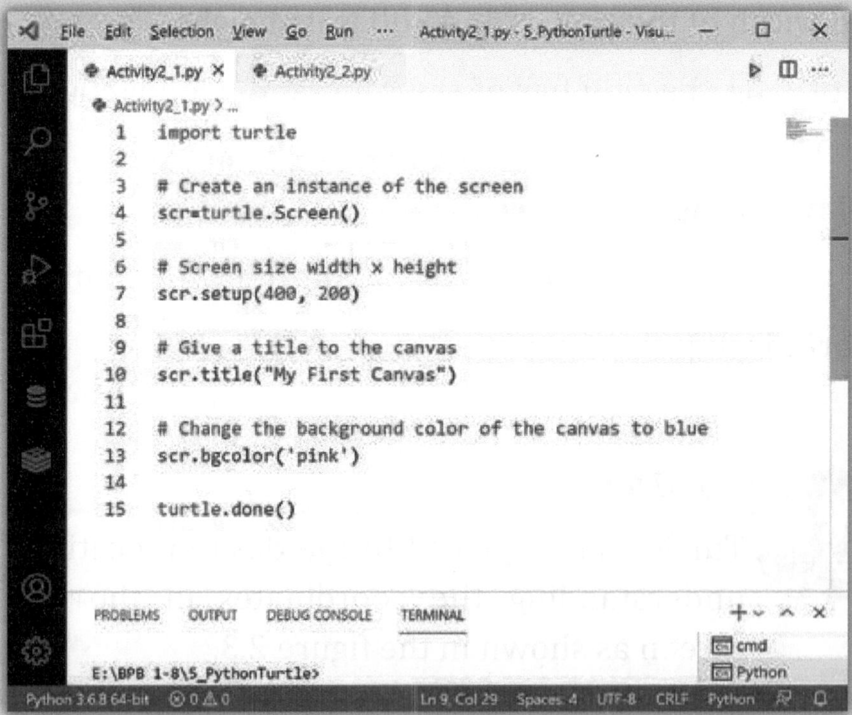

Figure 2.2(b): Code window for Activity 2.1

Activity 2.2

Write the code to add a text "Welcome to the world of programming using turtle" in the above activity 2.1 as shown in figure 2.2 (a).

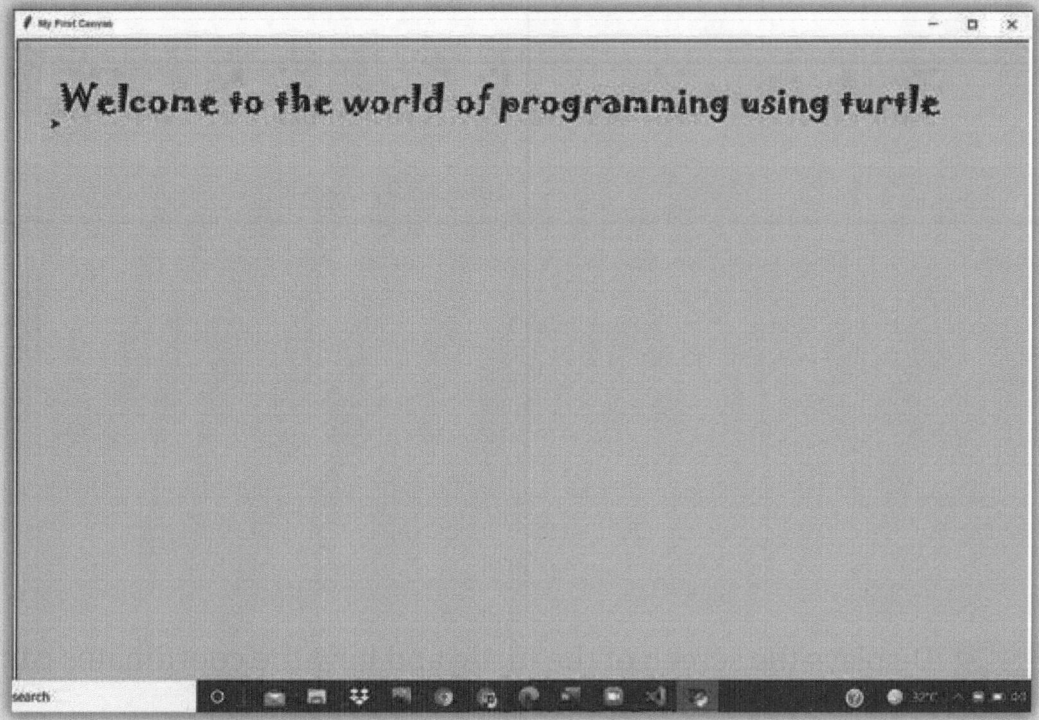

Figure 2.2(a): Output window for Activity 2.2

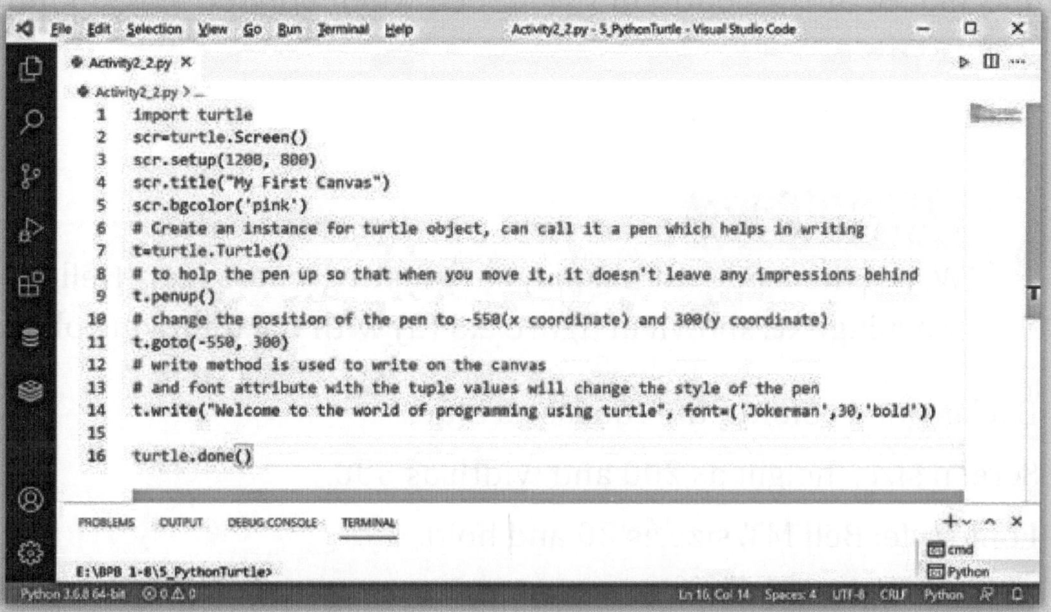

Figure 2.2(b): Code window for Activity 2.2

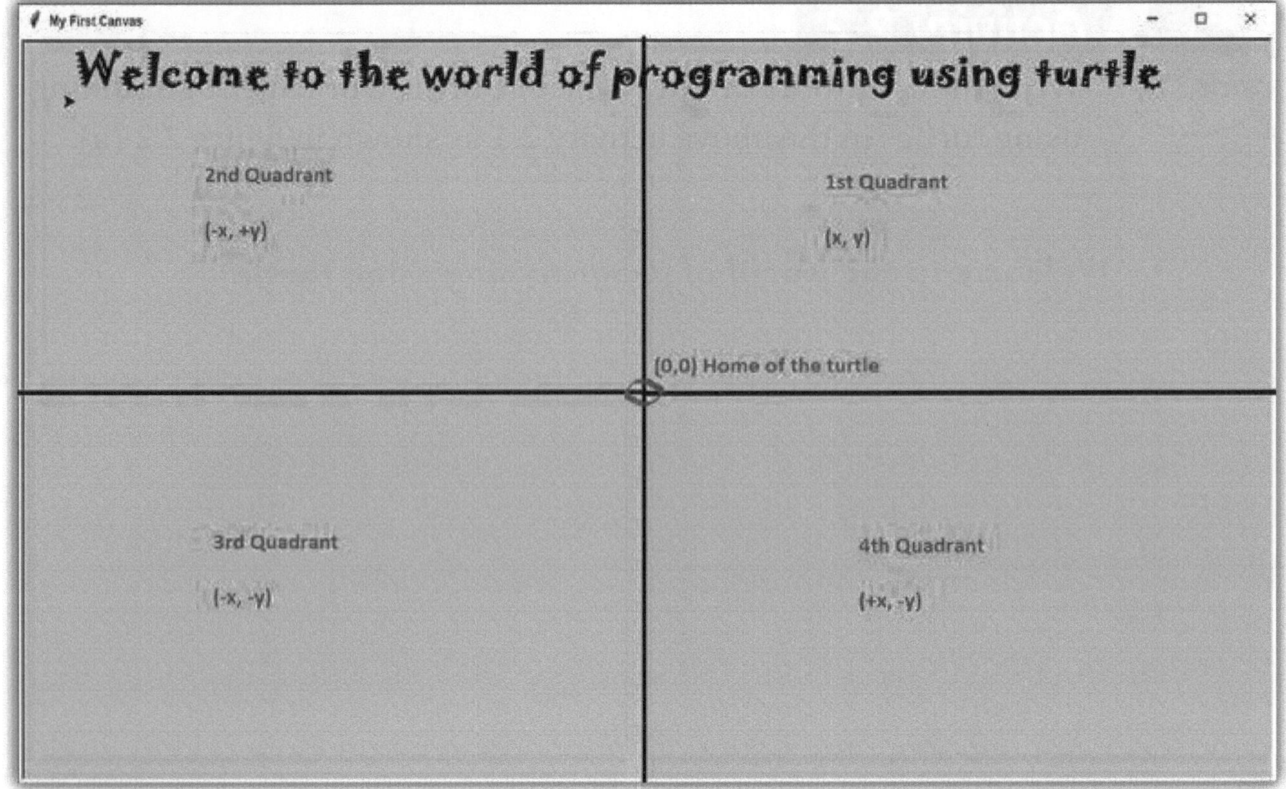

Figure 2.3: Displays the screen of the turtle and how the coordinates can be used

The turtle is placed at the centre of the screen when created and is known as the **home of the turtle**.

Activity 2.3

Write the code to display a greeting message "Hello!! Good morning!" as shown in figure 2.3 (a) with the following objectives:

- Background color of the canvas as blue.
- Screen size: height as 200 and width as 500.
- Font style: Bell MT, size as 20 and bold.
- Color of the text as Yellow.

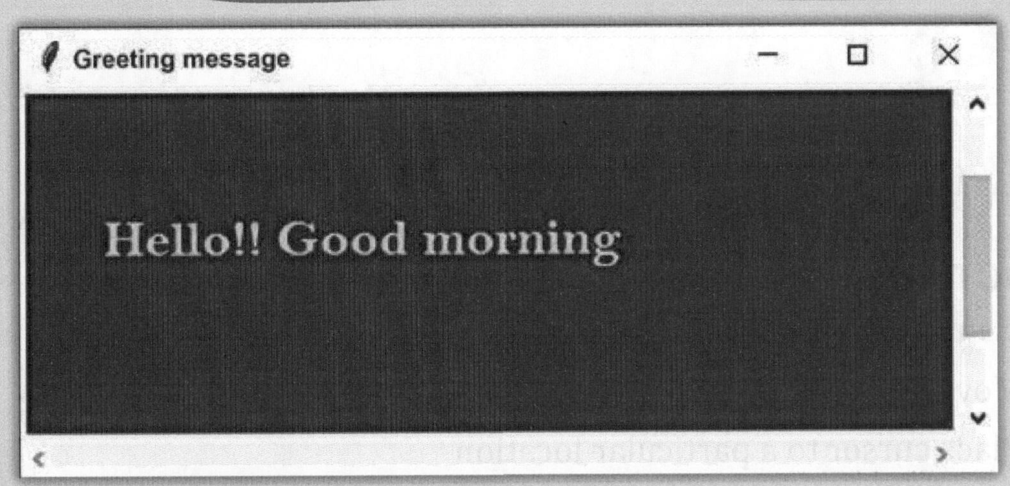

Figure 2.3(a): Output window for Activity 2.3

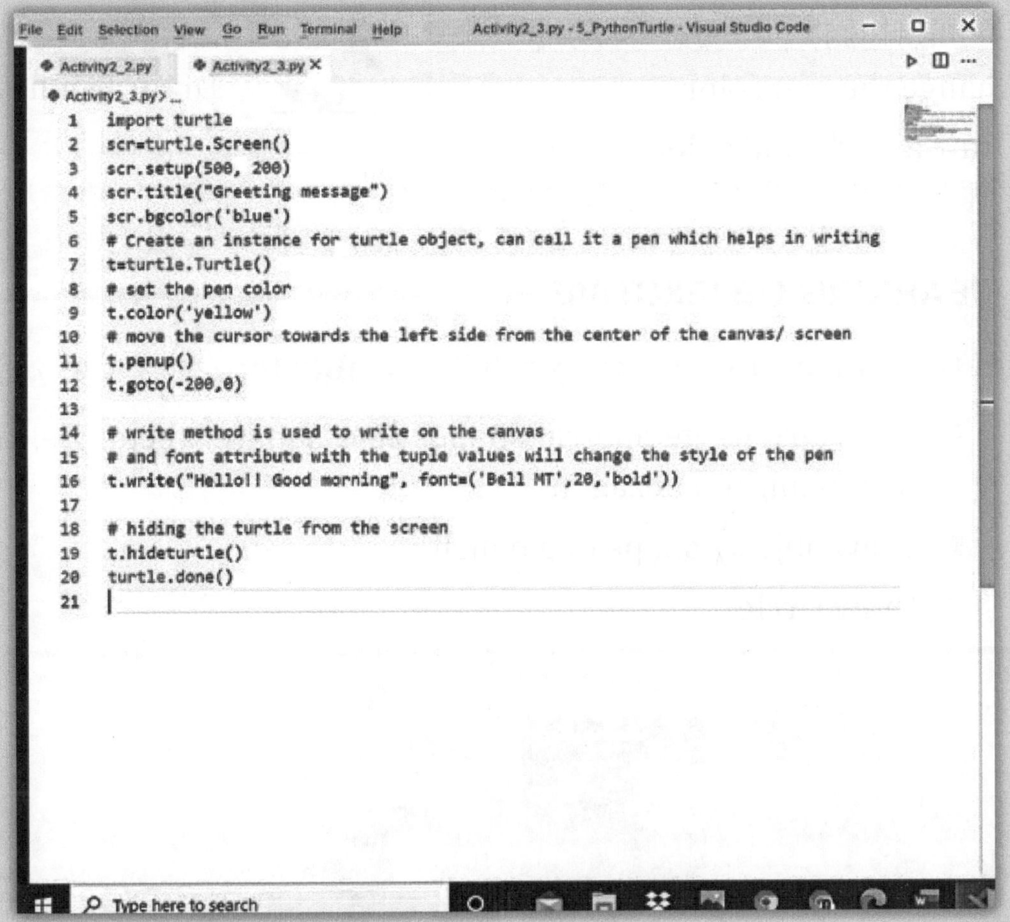

Figure 2.3(b): Code window for Activity 2.3

Playing with Shapes

STRUCTURE

In this chapter, you will learn and practice the following concepts:

- Move and draw
- Place cursor to a particular location
- Change the angle
- Fill object with a particular color
- Change the pen thickness / width
- Change the pen color
- Draw a circle and a dot

PROJECT

Draw a smiley

LEARNING OBJEXCTIVE

At the end of this chapter, you will be able to:

- Draw arious geometric shapes like square, rectangle, triangle, pentagon, and hexagon
- Draw object/ shape of a pencil
- Draw circle

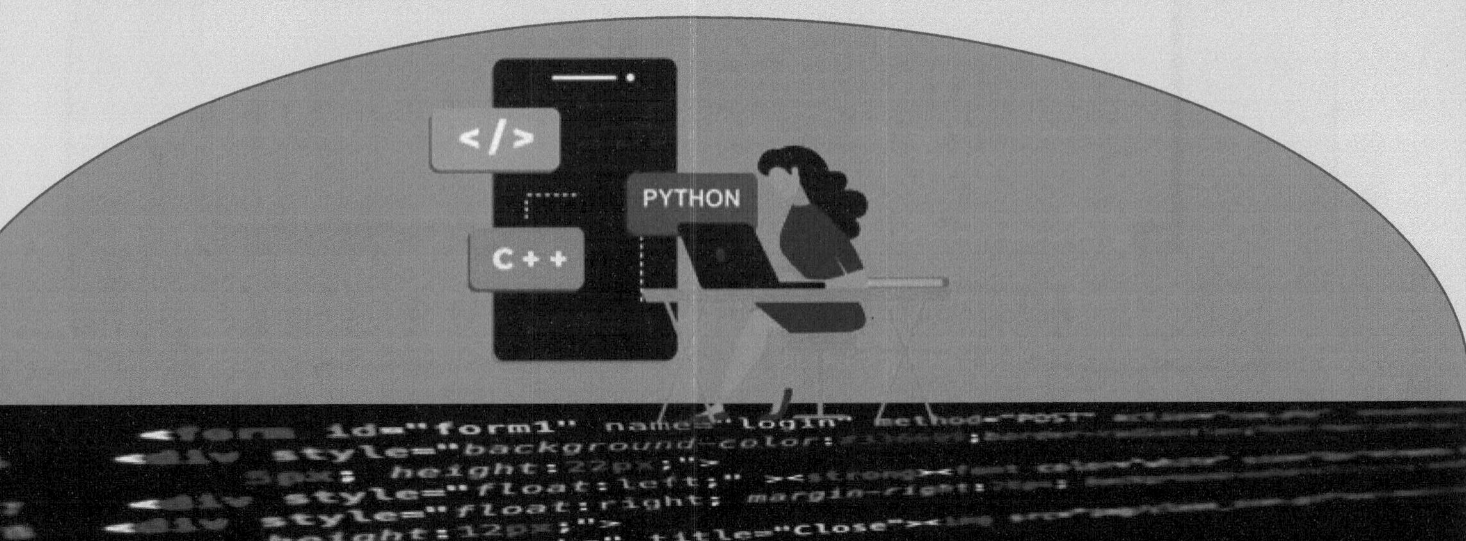

Turtle Commands

- **Turtle.Forward(steps) or turtle.FD(steps):** To move the turtle forward by a specified number of steps.
- **Turtle.Left(degree) or Turtle.Right(degree):** To change the direction of the turtle by the specified angle.
- **Turtle.goto(x,y):** To position the turtle to the point specified by x and y coordinates.
- **Turtle.penup() or turtle.pu():** Used when the impression of the turtle is not being left on the canvas while moving the turtle.
- **Turtle.color(code):** Choose the color of the turtle.
- **Turtle.fillcolor(code):** Choose the color with which the shape needs to be filled with.
- **Turtle.begin_fill():** To start the shape to be filled with the color chosen with turtle.fillcolor().
- **Turtle.end_fill():** To mark the end of the shape to be filled with a specific color.
- **Turtle.circle():** To draw the circle with the given radius.
- **Turtle.dot():** To draw the circle with filled color.

Info Bot

Dot() is used to draw the dot with the given diameter and the color to be filled with. Circle() is used to draw the circle with the given radius.

Activity 3.1

Write the code to draw a square and fill the shape with yellow color as shown in the figure 3.1(a) without filling the shape and figure 3.1(b) having the shape filled with yellow color..

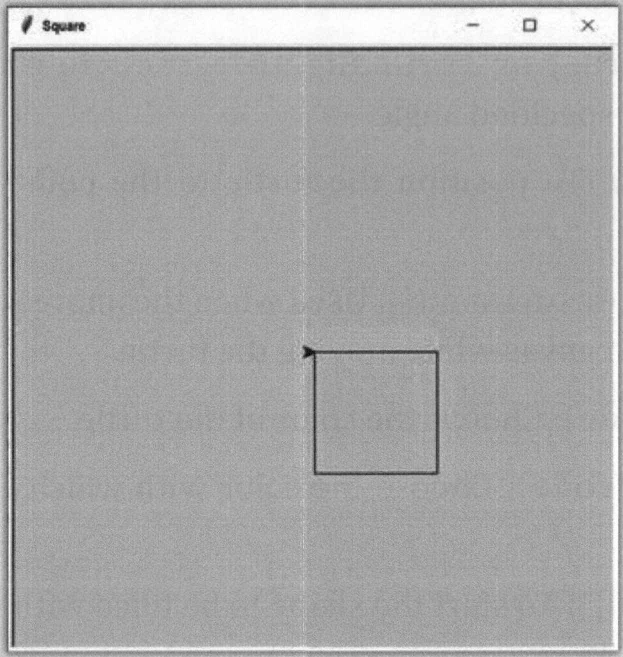

Figure 3.1(a): Output window for Activity 3.1 to display the square which is not filled with any color

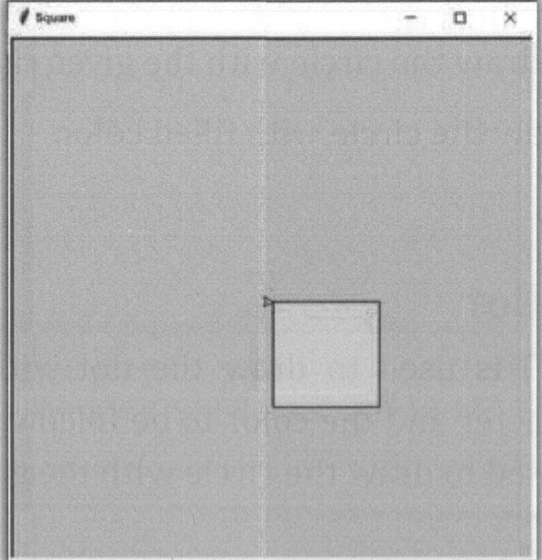

Figure 3.1(b): Output window for Activity 3.1

Figure 3.1(c): Code window for Activity 3.1 without filling the square with any color

Figure 3.1(d): Code window for Activity 3.1 by filling the square with yellow color

Practical 3.1 Write the code to draw a rectangle of width 100 and height 200. Fill it with blue color as shown in the figure 3.2.

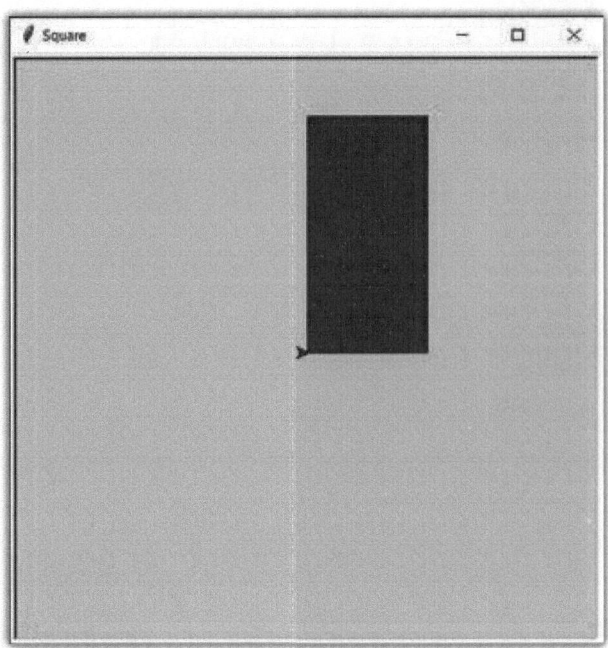

Figure 3.2: Output window for Practice 3.1

Activity 3.2

Write the code to draw a triangle. Fill the shape with purple color as shown in figure 3.2(a).

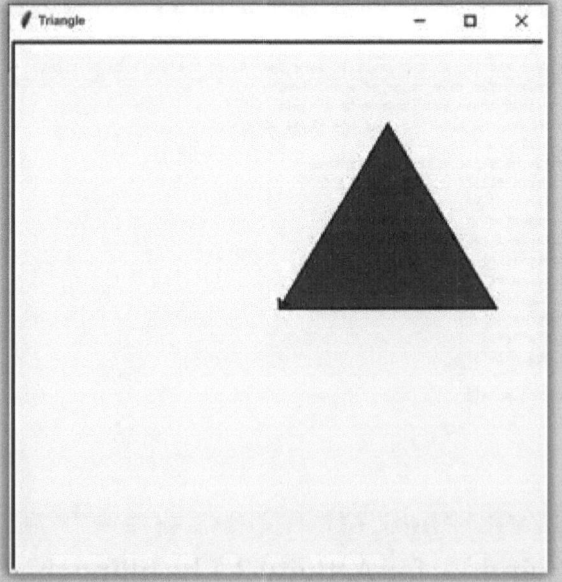

Figure 3.3(b): Output window for Activity 3.2

Figure 3.3(b): Code window for Activity 3.2

Info Bot

Angle sum property for a triangle is 180. Each angle in an equilateral triangle is 60 degrees. When the turtle has to take the turn and internal angle is 60, therefore external angle with which the turtle has to take turn is 120 degrees. The linear angle property is 180 degrees.

Activity 3.3

Write the code to draw a regular pentagon. Fill the shape with red color as shown in figure 3.4(a).

Info Bot

Regular pentagon has five equal sides with equal angles. To find the sum angle for a regular polygon is (n-2)*180.

For regular pentagon, the angle sum property is (5-2)*180 = 540.

Now, divide 540 by 5 and you get 108 degrees.

Therefore, all the internal angles are of measure 108 degrees.

The turtle has to take the turn of 72 degrees as the external angle is calculated as 180 minus 108 which is equal to 72 degrees.

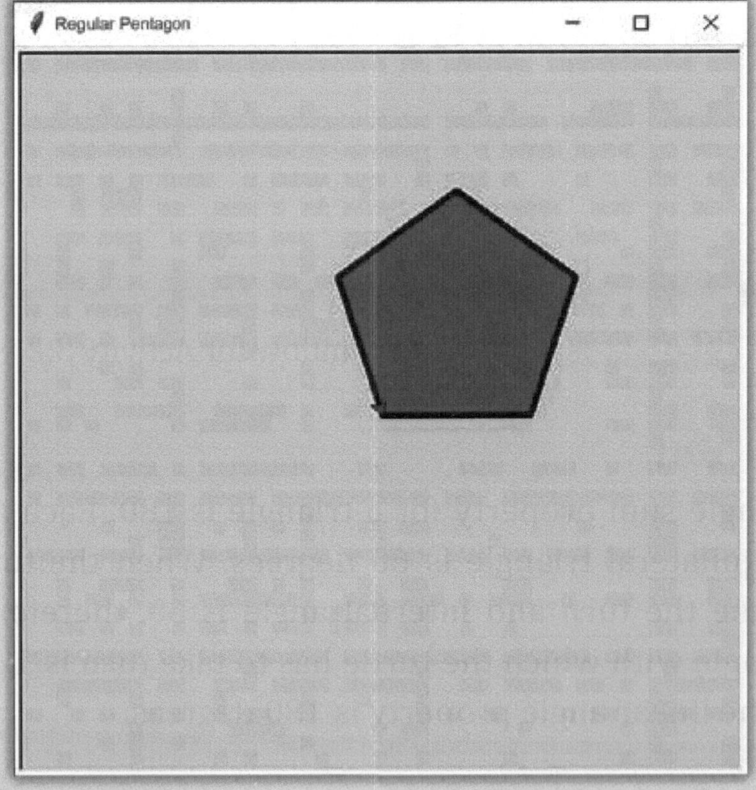

Figure 3.4(a): Output window for Activity 3.3

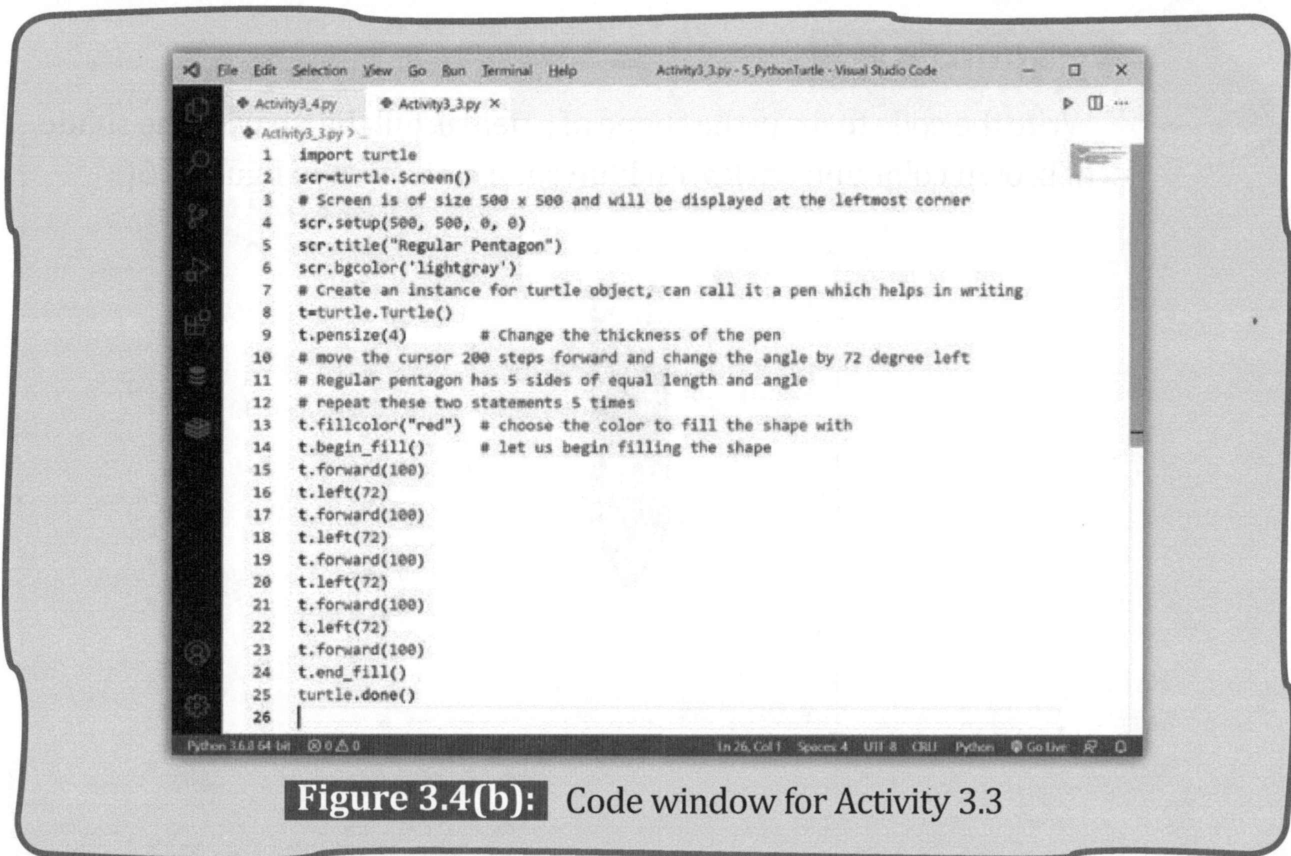

Figure 3.4(b): Code window for Activity 3.3

Practical 3.2 Write the code to draw a regular hexagon as shown in the figure 3.5

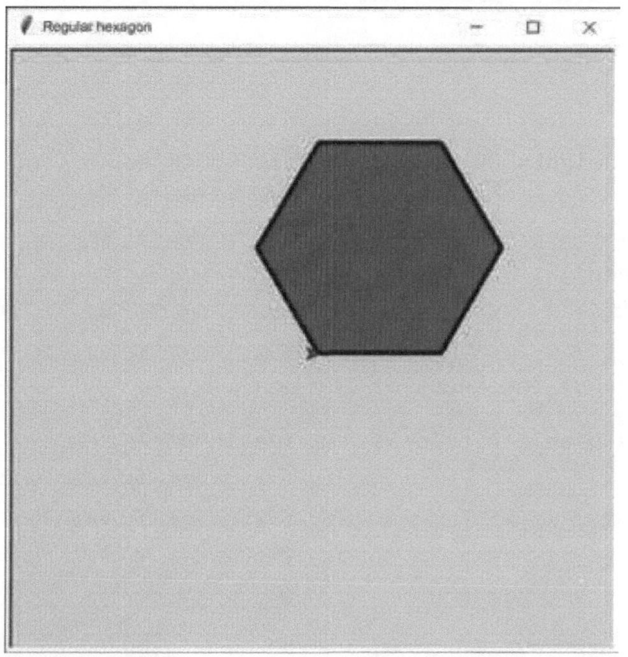

Figure 3.5: Output window for Practice 3.2

Activity 3.4

Write the code to draw the shape of a pencil. Fill the tip with the shade of brown color and back with blue color as shown in figure 3.6(a).

Figure 3.6(a): Output window for Activity 3.4

```
import turtle
scr=turtle.Screen()
scr.setup(width=600, height=600) # Screen size 600 x 600
scr.title("CIRCLE")
scr.bgcolor('lightgreen')
t=turtle.Turtle()   # Instance of turtle
t.pensize(3)        # Set thickness of the pen
t.circle(50)        # Draw a circle with a specified radius
t.penup()
t.goto(-100,150)
t.pendown()
t.circle(50, 180)   # semicircle in clockwise direction
```

```
t.penup()
t.goto(100,150)
t.pendown()
# semicircle in anticlockwise dir using radius negative
t.circle(-50,180)
t.penup()
t.goto(-40,-100)
t.pendown()
# creating an arc
t.right(60)
t.circle(50, 130)
turtle.done()
```

Figure 3.6(a): Output window for Activity 3.4

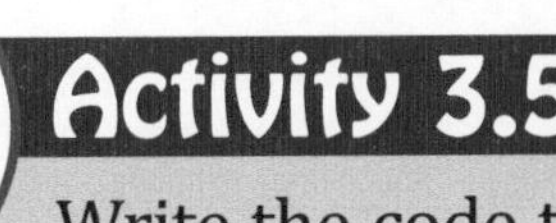

Activity 3.5

Write the code to draw the circle and arcs using turtle command as shown in figure 3.7(a).

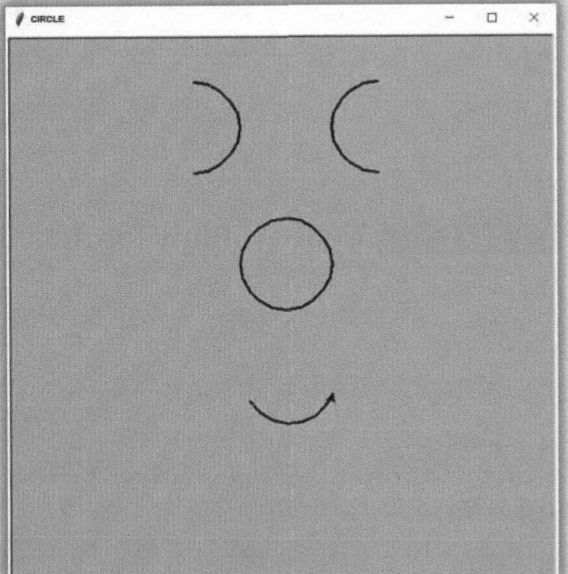

Figure 3.7(a): Output window for Activity 3.5

```
import turtle
scr=turtle.Screen()
scr.setup(width=600, height=600) # Screen size 600 x 600
scr.title("CIRCLE")
scr.bgcolor('lightgreen')
t=turtle.Turtle()    # Instance of turtle
t.pensize(3)         # Set thickness of the pen
t.circle(50)         # Draw a circle with a specified radius
t.penup()
t.goto(-100,150)
t.pendown()
t.circle(50, 180)    # semicircle in clockwise direction
t.penup()
t.goto(100,150)
t.pendown()
# semicircle in anticlockwise dir using radius negative
t.circle(-50,180)
t.penup()
t.goto(-40,-100)
t.pendown()
# creating an arc
t.right(60)
t.circle(50, 130)
turtle.done()
```

Figure 3.7(b): Code window for Activity 3.3

Activity 3.6

Write the code to draw the circle with filled color using turtle dot command as shown in figure 3.8(a).

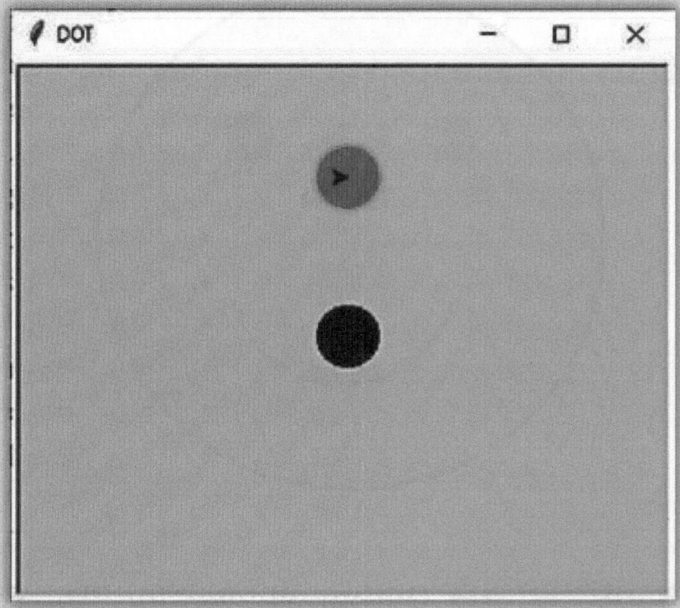

Figure 3.8(a): Output window for Activity 3.6

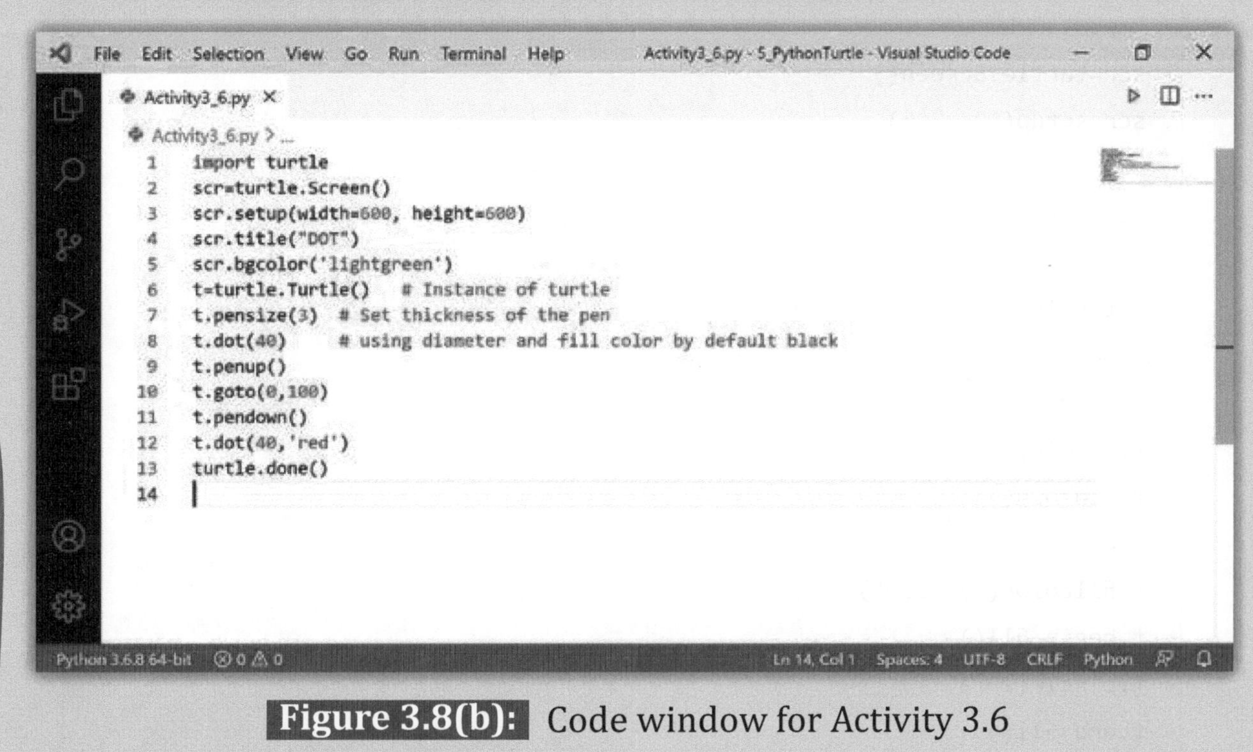

Figure 3.8(b): Code window for Activity 3.6

PROJECT: DRAW A SMILEY

Figure 3.9(a): Output window for Project

```
import turtle
scr=turtle.Screen()
scr.setup(800,500)

scr.title("Smiley Emoji")

t=turtle.Turtle()
t.pensize(4)
t.penup()
t.goto(0,-200)
t.pendown()
# face
t.fillcolor("yellow")
t.begin_fill()
t.circle(200)
t.end_fill()
# eyes
```

```
t.penup()
t.goto(-80,80)
t.pendown()
t.dot(40)
t.penup()
t.goto(80,80)
t.pendown()
t.dot(40)
t.penup()
t.goto(-80,-50)
t.pendown()
t.right(75)
t.circle(90,150)
t.ht()
turtle.done()
```

Figure 3.9(b): Code window for Project

Looping

STRUCTURE

In this chapter, you will learn and practice the following concepts:

- Geometric shapes
- Regular polygons
- Star
- Circle
- Project –Draw a house

LEARNING OBJEXCTIVE

- At the end of this chapter, you will be able to:
- Draw the shapes created in the previous chapter using for loop

Activity 4.1

Write the code to draw the square using for loop as shown in figure 4.1(a).

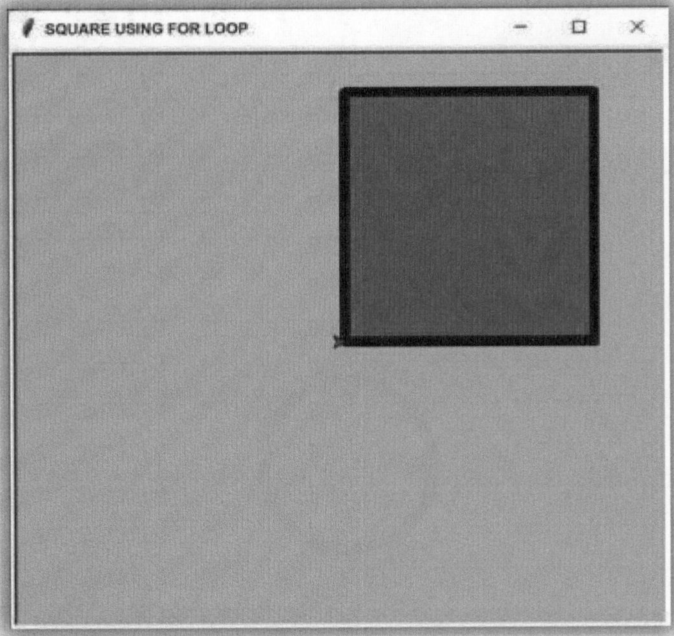

Figure 4.1(a): Output window for Activity 4.1

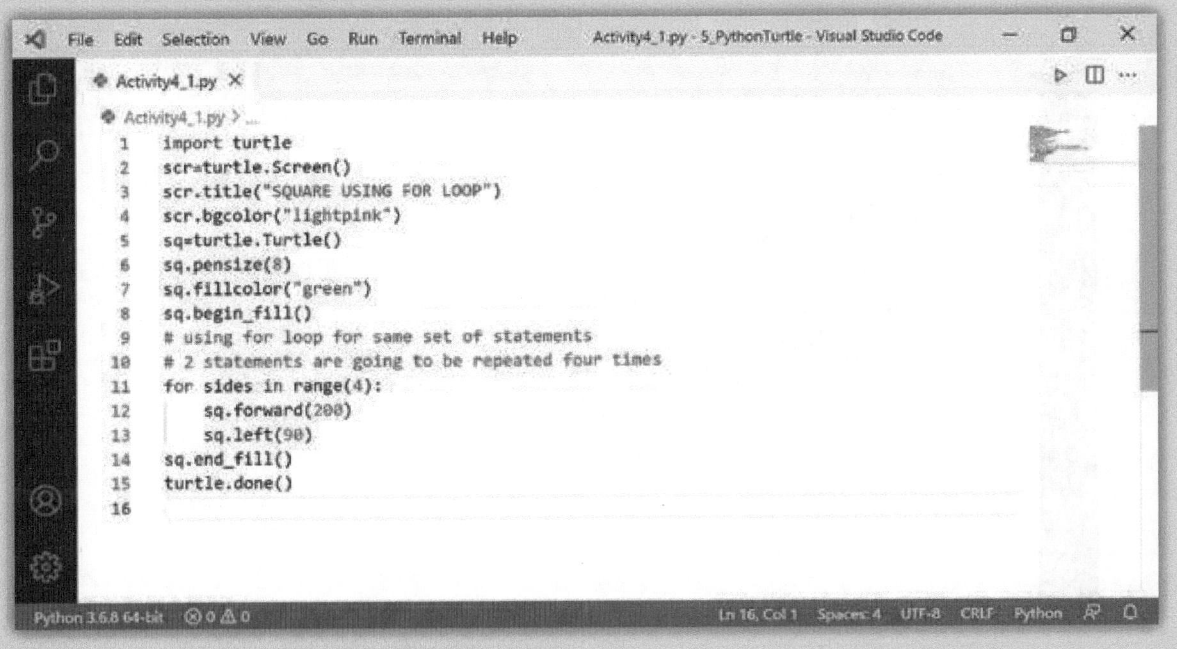

Figure 4.1(b): Code window for Activity 4.1

Activity 4.2

Write the code to draw a circle using for loop as shown in figure 4.2(a).

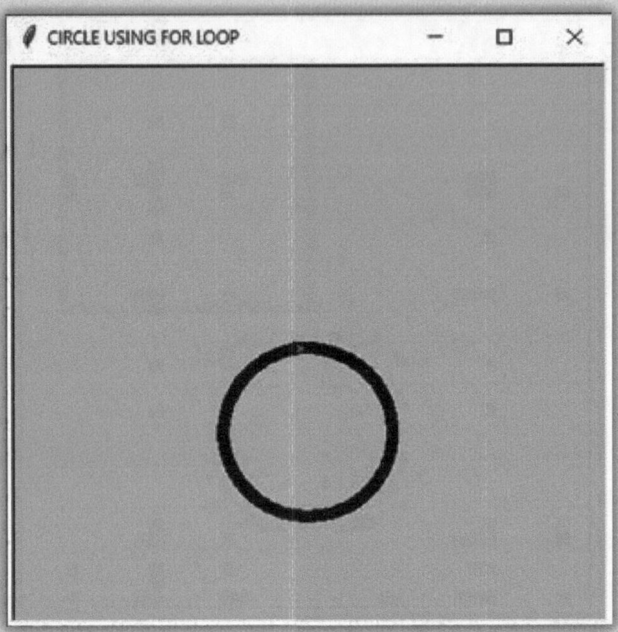

Figure 4.2(a): Output window for Activity 4.2

Figure 4.2(b): Code window for Activity 4.2

Activity 4.3

Write the code to draw a regular pentagon using for loop in figure 4.3(a).

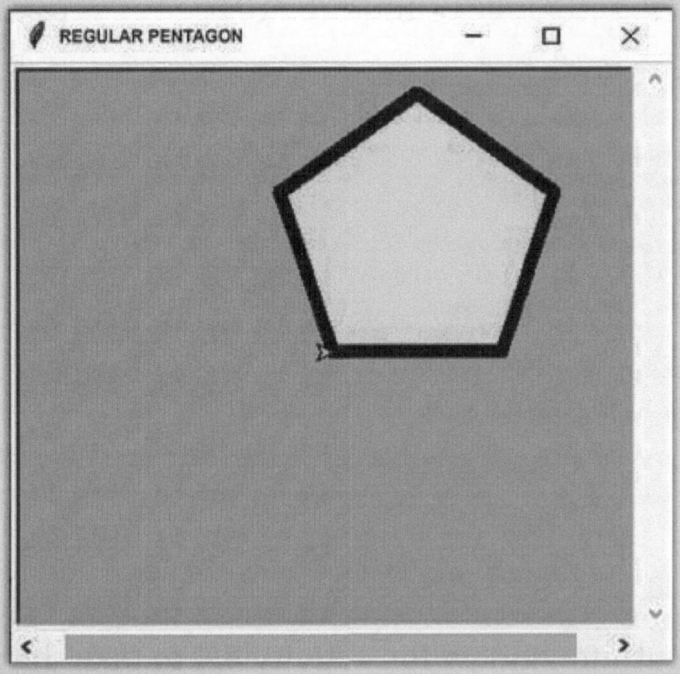

Figure 4.3(a): Output window for Activity 4.3

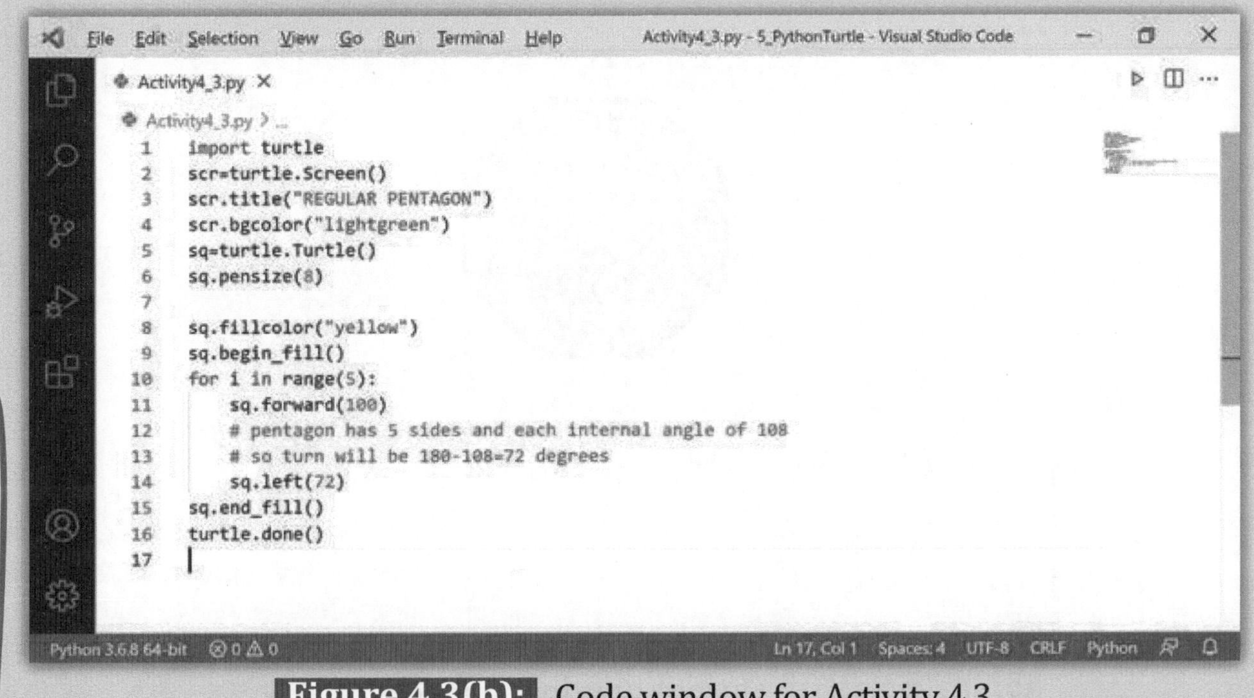

Figure 4.3(b): Code window for Activity 4.3

Activity 4.4

Write the code to read the number of sides from the user to draw a regular polygon based on number of sides as shown in figure 4.4(a) and figure 4.4(b).

Figure 4.4(a): Output window for Activity 4.4 to take the input for number of sides for the regular pentagon

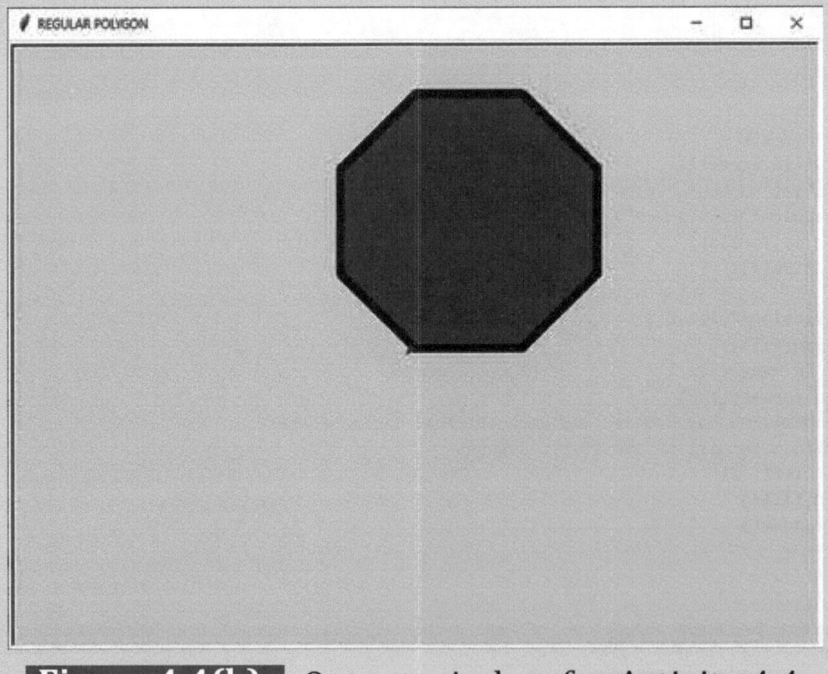

Figure 4.4(b): Output window for Activity 4.4

```
import turtle
scr=turtle.Screen()
scr.title("REGULAR POLYGON")
scr.bgcolor("lightgrey")
sq=turtle.Turtle()
sq.pensize(8)
# take the number of sides from the user for regular polygon
sides=int(input("Enter number of sides? "))
# Calculate the angle sum property for the regular polygon
angles=(sides-2)*180
# calculate each angle of the shape
angle=angles/sides
# calculate the exterior angle using linear angle property
ext_ang=180-angle
# Use of for loop to draw the polygon
sq.fillcolor("blue")
sq.begin_fill()
for i in range(sides):
    sq.forward(100)
    sq.left(ext_ang)
sq.end_fill()
turtle.done()
```

Figure 4.4(b): Code window for Activity 4.4

Activity 4.5

Write the code to draw a star using for loop as shown in figure 4.5(a).

Figure 4.5(a): Output window for Activity 4.5

```python
import turtle
scr=turtle.Screen()
scr.title("STAR")
scr.bgcolor("lightblue")
sq=turtle.Turtle()
sq.pensize(8)
# take the number of sides from the user for regular polygon

sq.fillcolor("grey")
sq.begin_fill()
for i in range(5):
    sq.forward(200)
    # internal angle 36 degree
    # turn 180-36= 144 degrees
    # 2 triangles makes a star
    # sum property of a triangle is 180
    sq.left(144)
sq.end_fill()
turtle.done()
```

Figure 4.5(b): Code window for Activity 4.5

Activity 4.6

Write the code to draw six stars in a horizontal line with six different colors from a list of colors as shown in figure 4.6(a).

Figure 4.6(a): Output window for Activity 4.6

```
import turtle
scr=turtle.Screen()
scr.title("Line of stars")
scr.bgcolor("lightgrey")
tur=turtle.Turtle()
tur.pensize(4)
col=['red','blue','orange','yellow','purple','brown']  # list of colors
# for loop for 6 stars
x,y=-300,0
for i in range(6):
    tur.fillcolor(col[i]) # pick color one by one
    tur.begin_fill()
    tur.penup()
    tur.goto(x,y)
    x+=100
    tur.pendown()
    # draw a star
    for i in range(5):
        tur.forward(80)
        tur.right(144)
    tur.end_fill()

turtle.done()
```

Figure 4.6(b): Code window for Activity 4.6

PROJECT – Create a shape of house using turtle commands practiced so far as shown in figure 4.7(a).

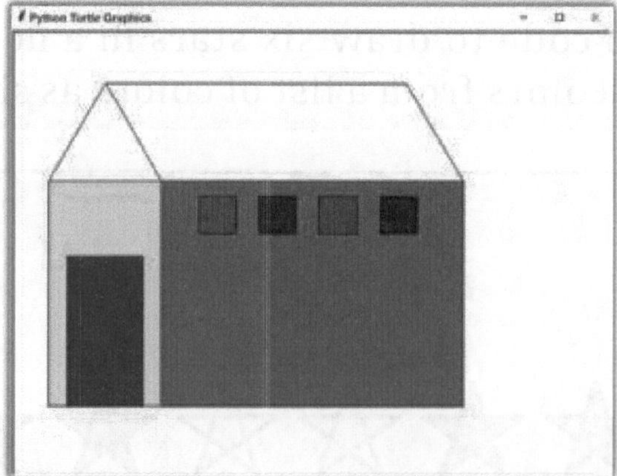

Figure 4.7(a): Output window for Project

```
import turtle

scr=turtle.Screen()
scr.setup(800,600)
t=turtle.Turtle()

t.pu()
t.goto(-200,-200)
t.pd()
t.fillcolor('grey')
t.begin_fill()
for i in range(2):
  t.forward(400)
  t.lt(90)
  t.forward(300)
  t.lt(90)
t.end_fill()
t.pu()
t.goto(-350,-200)
t.pd()
t.fillcolor('yellow')
t.begin_fill()
for i in range(2):
  t.forward(150)
  t.lt(90)
  t.forward(300)
  t.lt(90)
t.end_fill()
t.pu()
t.goto(-325,-200)
t.pd()
t.fillcolor('brown')
t.begin_fill()
for i in range(2):
  t.forward(100)
  t.lt(90)
  t.forward(200)
  t.lt(90)
t.end_fill()

t.pu()
t.goto(-350,100)
t.pd()
t.lt(60)
t.fd(150)
t.rt(120)
t.fd(150)
t.goto(-275,230)
t.goto(125,230)
t.goto(200,100)
t.right(30)
t.pu()
t.goto(-100,80)
t.pd()
t.fillcolor('green')
t.begin_fill()
for i in range(4):
  t.forward(50)
  t.rt(90)
t.end_fill()

  t.pu()
t.goto(-20,80)
t.pd()
t.fillcolor('blue')
t.begin_fill()
for i in range(4):
  t.forward(50)
  t.rt(90)
t.end_fill()

t.pu()
t.goto(60,80)
t.pd()
t.fillcolor('green')
t.begin_fill()
for i in range(4):
  t.forward(50)
  t.rt(90)
t.end_fill()

t.pu()
t.goto(140,80)
t.pd()
t.fillcolor('blue')
t.begin_fill()
for i in range(4):
  t.forward(50)
  t.rt(90)
t.end_fill()
t.hideturtle()

turtle.done()
```

Figure 4.7(b): Code window for Project

5 Random Module

STRUCTURE

In this chapter, you will learn and practice the following concepts:

- Drawing shapes at random locations
- Drawing shapes with random colours at random locations
- Project –Draw a random number of stars with random colors

LEARNING OBJEXCTIVE

At the end of this chapter, you will be able to:

- Display the shapes at random locations, with random colors

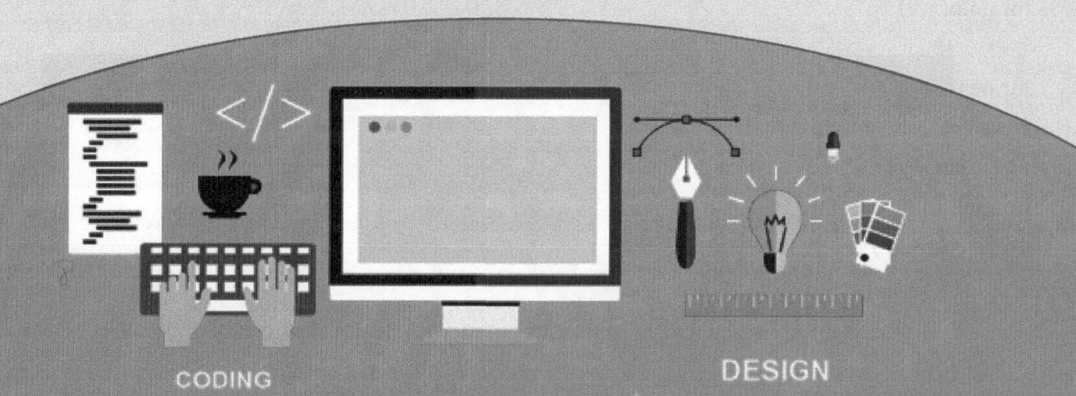

Activity 5.1

Write the code to draw ten circles in a horizontal line with random colors from the list of colors as shown in figure 5.1(a)

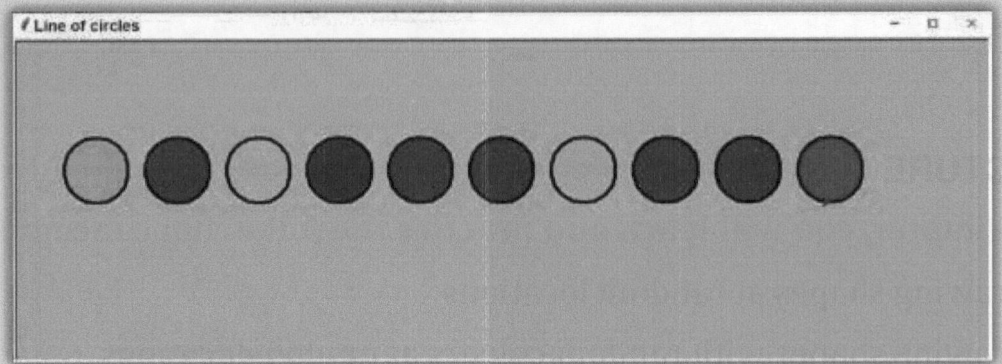

Figure 5.1(a): Output window for Activity 5.1

```
import turtle
import random
scr=turtle.Screen()
scr.setup(1200,400)
scr.title("Line of circles")
scr.bgcolor("light pink")
tur=turtle.Turtle()
tur.pensize(4)
col=['red','blue','orange','yellow','pur-
ple','brown','light green','sky blue']# list of colors
x, y = -500, 0
for i in range(10):
  tur.fillcolor(random.choice(col))
# pick randomly color from the list of colors
  tur.begin_fill()
  tur.penup()
  tur.goto(x,y)
  x += 100
  tur.pendown()
  # draw a circle
  tur.circle(40)
  tur.end_fill()
turtle.done()
```

Figure 5.1(b): Code window for Activity 5.1

Activity 5.2

Write the code to draw ten stars in a diagonal line with random colors as shown in figure 5.2(a).

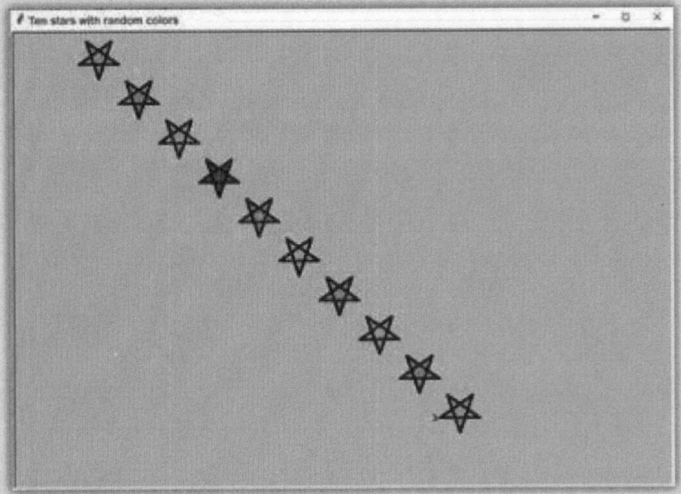

Figure 5.2(a): Output window for Activity 5.2

```
import turtle
import random
scr=turtle.Screen()
scr.setup(1000,700)
scr.title("Ten stars with random colors")
scr.bgcolor("light pink")
scr.colormode(255)
tur=turtle.Turtle()
tur.pensize(4)
x, y = -400, 300
for i in range(10):
  r = random.randint(0,255)
  g = random.randint(0,255)
  b = random.randint(0,255)
  tur.fillcolor(r,g,b)
  tur.begin_fill()
  tur.penup()
  tur.goto(x,y)
x += 60
  y -= 60
  tur.pendown()
# draw a star
  for a in range(5):
    tur.forward(60)
    tur.left(144)
  tur.end_fill()
turtle.done()
```

Figure 5.2(b): Code window for Activity 5.2

PROJECT – Draw a random number of stars with random colors as shown in figure 5.3(a)

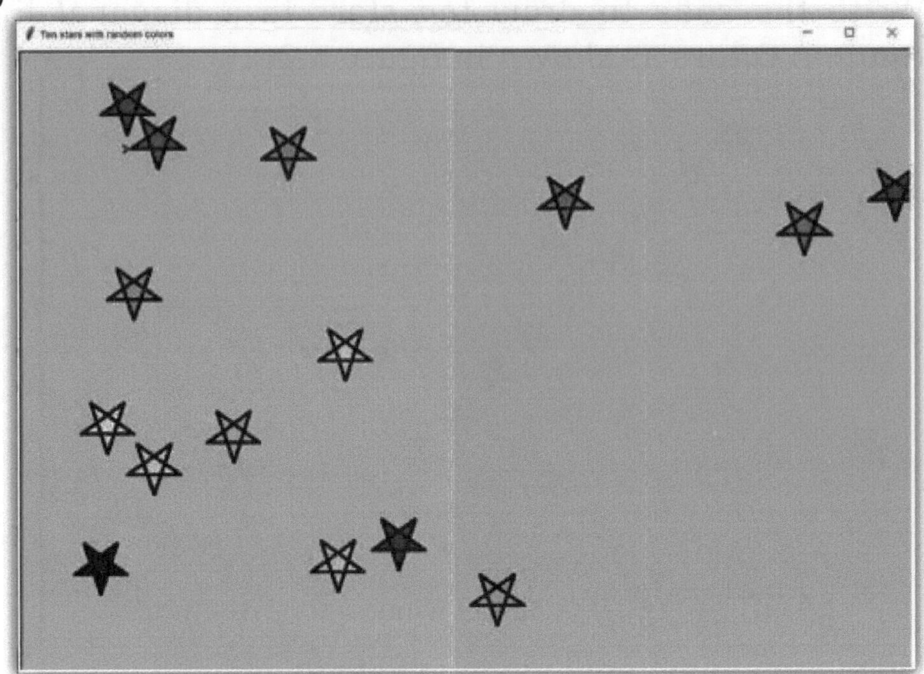

Figure 5.3(a): Output window for Project

```
import turtle
import random
scr=turtle.Screen()
scr.setup(1000,700)
scr.title("Ten stars with ran-
dom colors")
scr.bgcolor("light pink")
scr.colormode(255)
tur=turtle.Turtle()
tur.pensize(4)
# random starts between 10 and 30
for i in range(random.randint(10,30)):
  # random colors
  r = random.randint(0,255)
  g = random.randint(0,255)
  b = random.randint(0,255)
    tur.fillcolor(r,g,b)
tur.begin_fill()
  tur.penup()
# random positions
  x=random.randint(-450,450)
  y=random.randint(-300, 300)
  tur.goto(x,y)
  tur.pendown()
  # draw a star
  for a in range(5):
    tur.forward(60)
    tur.left(144)
  tur.end_fill()
turtle.done()
```

Figure 5.3(b): Code window for Project

6 User-defined Functions

STRUCTURE

In this chapter, you will learn and practice the following concepts:

- Write your own functions for creating different shapes
- Project –Draw a house using functions

LEARNING OBJEXCTIVE

At the end of this chapter, you will be able to:

- Create your own functions for a specific task and call it wherever it is required

Activity 6.1

Create a function to draw a star and then call this function star to draw it at ten random locations.

Figure 6.1(a): Output window for Activity 6.1

```
import turtle
import random
scr=turtle.Screen()
scr.setup(1000,700)
scr.title("Creating functions")
scr.bgcolor("light pink")
scr.colormode(255)
tur=turtle.Turtle()
tur.pensize(4)
# function to print star with size called
def star(size):
    for i in range(5):
        tur.forward(size)
        tur.left(144)

# for loop to draw 10 stars at random locations within the screen
for i in range(10):
    r = random.randint(0,255)
    g = random.randint(0,255)
    b = random.randint(0,255)
    x = random.randrange(-400, 400)
    y = random.randrange(-300, 300)
    tur.fillcolor(r,g,b) # pick randomly color from the list of colors
    tur.begin_fill()
    tur.penup()
    tur.goto(x,y)
    x += 60
    y -= 60
    tur.pendown()
    star(random.randint(30, 70)) # star with random side length between 30 to 70
    tur.end_fill()
turtle.done()
```

Figure 6.1(b): Code window for Activity 6.1

PROJECT – Draw a house by using the functions rectangle, triangle and circle.

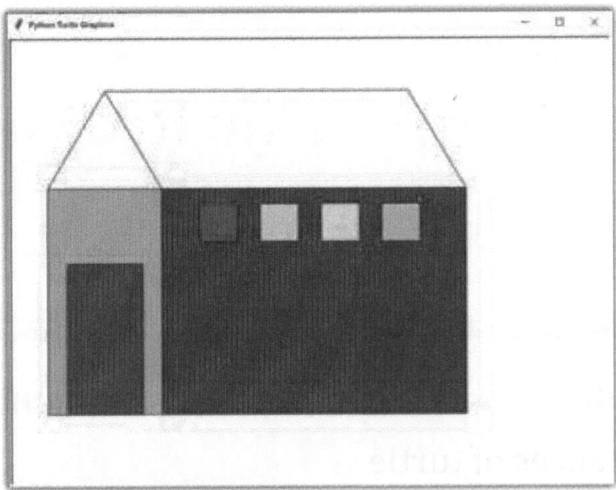

Figure 6.2(a): Output window for Project

```
import turtle

scr=turtle.Screen()
scr.setup(800,600)

t=turtle.Turtle()
# function to create rectangle
def rect(x,y,len,br,c):
  t.pu()
  t.goto(x,y)
  t.pd()
  t.fillcolor(c)
  t.begin_fill()
  for i in range(2):
    t.forward(len)
    t.lt(90)
    t.forward(br)
    t.lt(90)
  t.end_fill()
# function to create square
def sq(x,y,s,c):
  t.pu()
  t.goto(x,y)
  t.pd()
  t.fillcolor(c)
  t.begin_fill()
  for i in range(4):
    t.forward(s)
    t.rt(90)
  t.end_fill()
# calling functions rectangle
rect(-200,-200,400,300,'blue')
rect(-350,-200,150,300,'orange')
rect(-325,-200,100,200,'brown')
t.pu()
t.goto(-350,100)
t.pd()
t.lt(60)
t.fd(150)
t.rt(120)
t.fd(150)
t.goto(-275,230)
t.goto(125,230)
t.goto(200,100)
t.right(30)
# calling functions square
sq(-100,80,50,'red')
sq(-20,80,50,'light blue')
sq(60,80,50,'yellow')
sq(140,80,50,'silver')

turtle.done()
```

Figure 6.2(b): *Code window for Project*

7 Game – Turtle Race

STRUCTURE

In this chapter, you will learn and practice the following concepts:

- Using various instances of turtle
- Turtles with different colors
- Use of loop and conditional statement

LEARNING OBJEXCTIVE

At the end of this chapter, you will be able to:

- Build the screen to be displayed
- Add the racing track to the game
- Decide the number of turtles required to be in the race
- Position the turtles on the track
- Start the race
- Declare the winners
- Display the result of the game

Activity 7.1

Create the screen to display the heading on it "Turtle Racing", draw the track for the turtles to race.

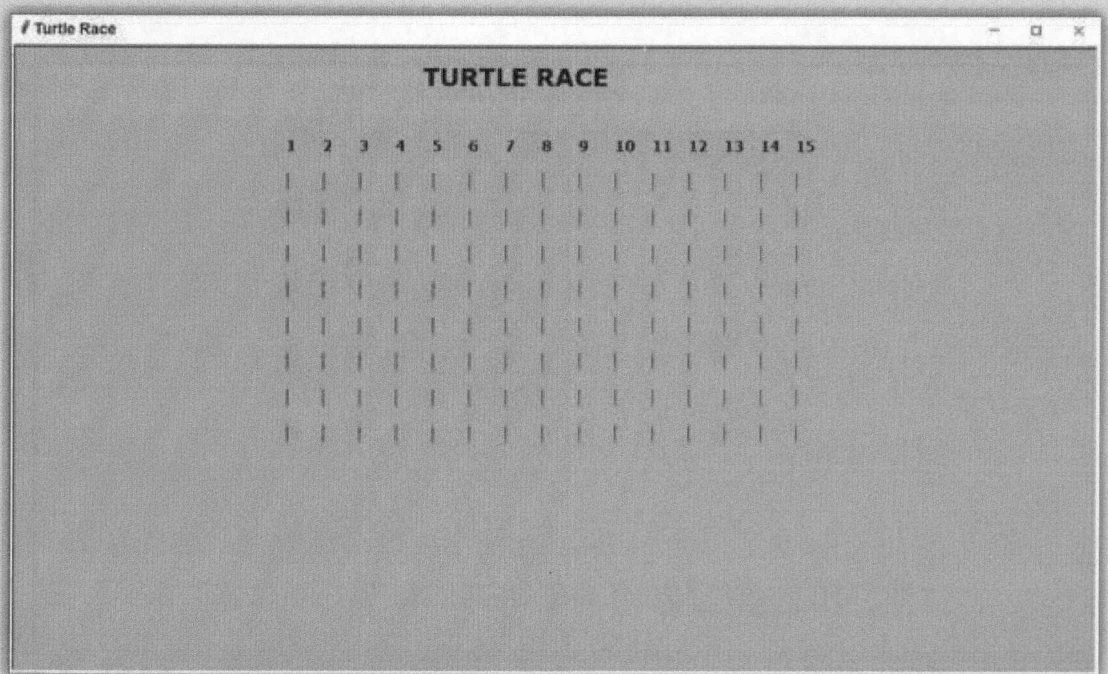

Figure 7.1(a): Output window for Activity 7.1

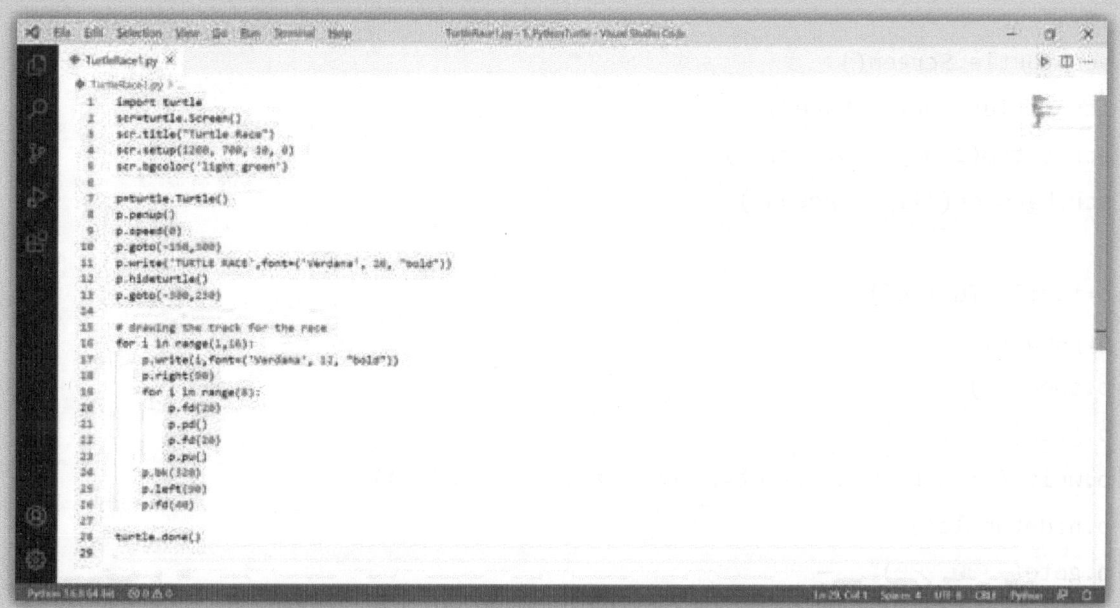

Figure 7.1(b): Code window for Activity 7.1

Activity 7.2

Add four turtles before the racing track in the above activity.

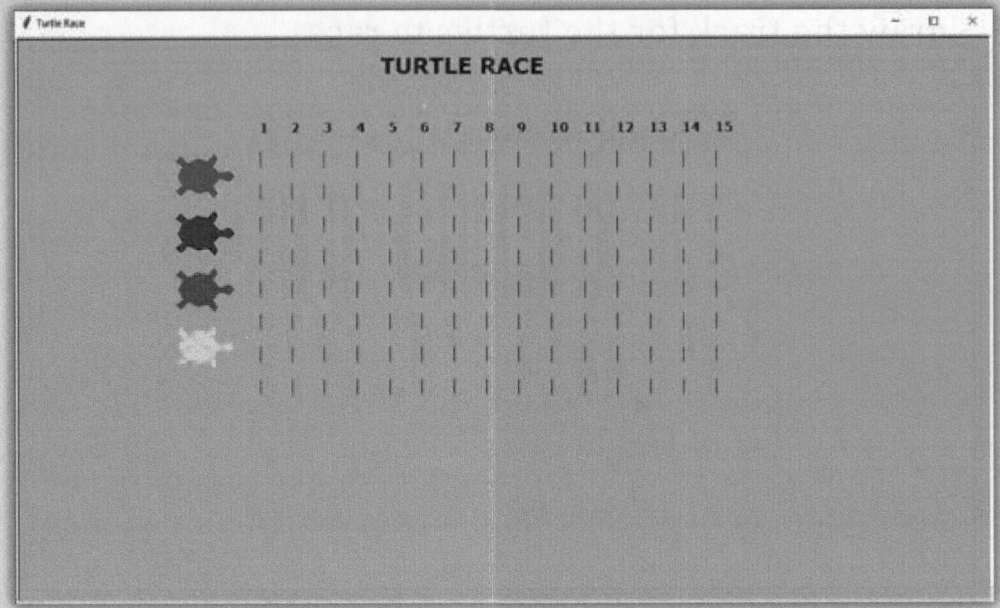

Figure 7.2(a): Output window for Activity 7.2

```
import turtle
import random

scr=turtle.Screen()
scr.title("Turtle Race")
scr.setup(1200, 700, 10, 0)
scr.bgcolor('light green')

p=turtle.Turtle()
p.penup()
p.speed(0)
p.goto(-150,300)
p.write('TURTLE RACE',font=('Verdana', 20, "bold"))
p.hideturtle()
p.goto(-300,230)
```

```
# drawing the track for the race
for i in range(1,16):
  p.write(i,font=('Verdana', 12, "bold"))
  p.right(90)
  for i in range(8):
    p.fd(20)
    p.pd()
    p.fd(20)
    p.pu()
  p.bk(320)
  p.left(90)
  p.fd(40)

# Creating 4 instances of turtle
red=turtle.Turtle()
blue=turtle.Turtle()
green=turtle.Turtle()
yellow=turtle.Turtle()

# Function to set the properties like color, shape, size, x, y coordi-
nates for the turtle
def create_tur(t,c,x,y):
  t.color(c)
  t.pu()
  t.shape('turtle')
  t.shapesize(3)
  t.goto(x,y)
  for i in range(4):
    t.left(90)
  t.pd()
```

Figure 7.2(b): Code window for Activity 7.2

Start the race in the above activity, also declare the Name of the winning turtle with the same color of the winning turtle.

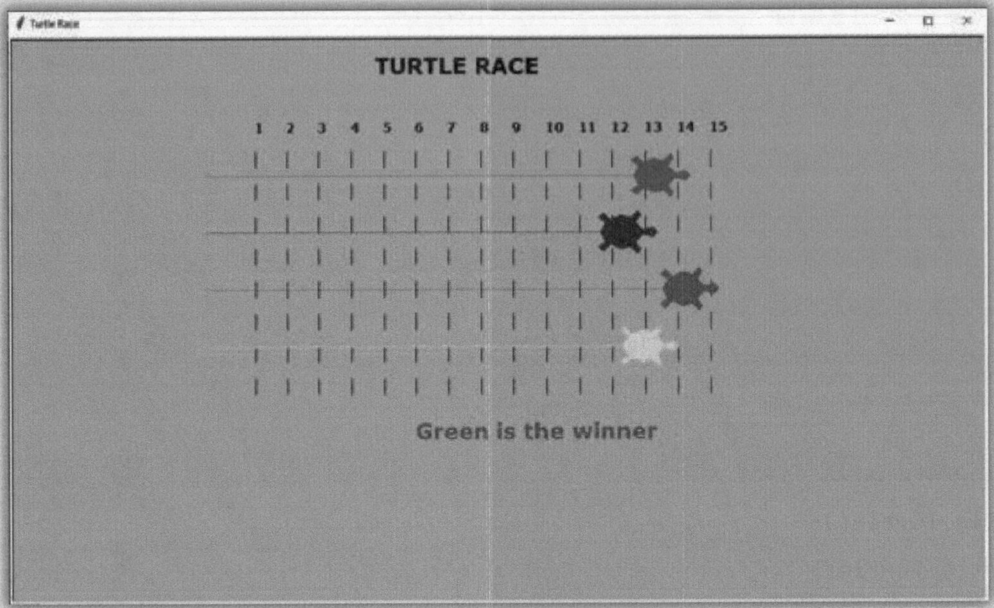

Figure 7.3(a): Output window for Activity 7.3

Add the following segment of code before the last line of the activity 7.2(b).

```
# Start the race
for i in range(100):
    red.forward(random.randint(1,10))
    blue.forward(random.randint(1,10))
    green.forward(random.randint(1,10))
    yellow.forward(random.randint(1,10))

p.goto(-100,-150)

# Finding the winner
if red.xcor()>blue.xcor() and red.xcor()>green.xcor() and red.xcor()>yellow.xcor():
    p.color("red")
    p.write("Red is the winner",font=('Verdana', 20, "bold"))
elif blue.xcor()>red.xcor() and blue.xcor()>green.xcor() and blue.xcor()>yellow.xcor():
    p.color("blue")
    p.write("Blue is the winner",font=('Verdana', 20, "bold"))
elif green.xcor()>red.xcor() and green.xcor()>blue.xcor() and green.xcor()>yellow.xcor():
    p.color("green")
    p.write("Green is the winner",font=('Verdana', 20, "bold"))
else:
    p.color("yellow")
    p.write("Yellow is the winner",font=('Verdana', 20, "bold"))

turtle.done()
```

Figure 7.3(b): Code window for Activity 7.1

Activity 7.4

Draw seven stars below the winner declaration with the same color as that of the winning turtle.

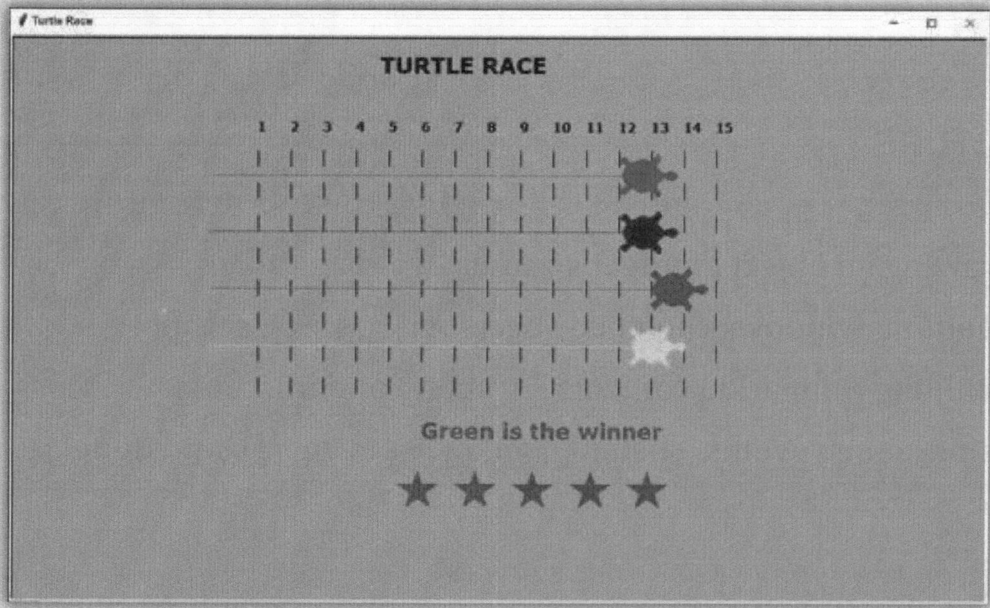

Figure 7.4(a): Output window for Activity 7.4

Add the following segment of code before the last line of activity 7.3(b)

```
        p.color("green")
        p.write("Green is the winner",font=('Verdana', 20, "bold"))
    else:
        p.color("yellow")
        p.write("Yellow is the winner",font=('Verdana', 20, "bold"))

# Function to draw the star
def star(x,y):
    p.goto(x,y)
    p.begin_fill()
    for i in range(5):
        p.fd(50)
        p.rt(144)
    p.end_fill()

# Draw 5 stars by calling the function using for loop
x, y = -130, -200
for i in range(5):
    star(x,y)
    x = x + 70

turtle.done()
```

Figure 7.4(b): Code window for Activity 7.4

Game – Fidget Spinner

STRUCTURE

In this chapter, you will learn and practice the following concepts:

- Drawing an object of fidget spinner
- Handling windows controls – bgcolor(), clear(), setup()
- Handling Animation controls – tracer() and update()
- Using screen events – listen(), onkey(),ontimer(), and done()

LEARNING OBJEXCTIVE

At the end of this chapter, you will be able to:

- Initialise the state of the drawing object, angles for rotating it
- Animate the fidget spinner by checking the condition of its state
- Install the timer to call the user-defined function animate() again and again after a specific time in milliseconds

Activity 8.1

Create the screen to display the heading on it as FIDGET SPINNER, draw the fidget as shown in figure 8.1(a).

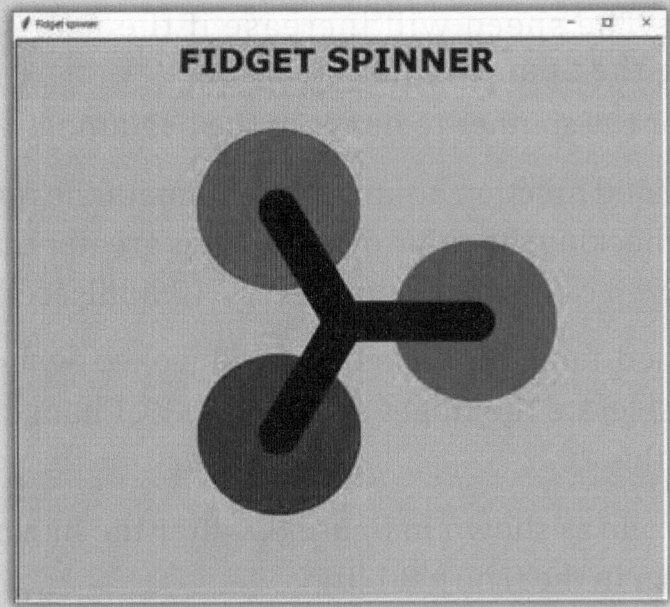

Figure 8.1(a): Output window for Activity 8.1

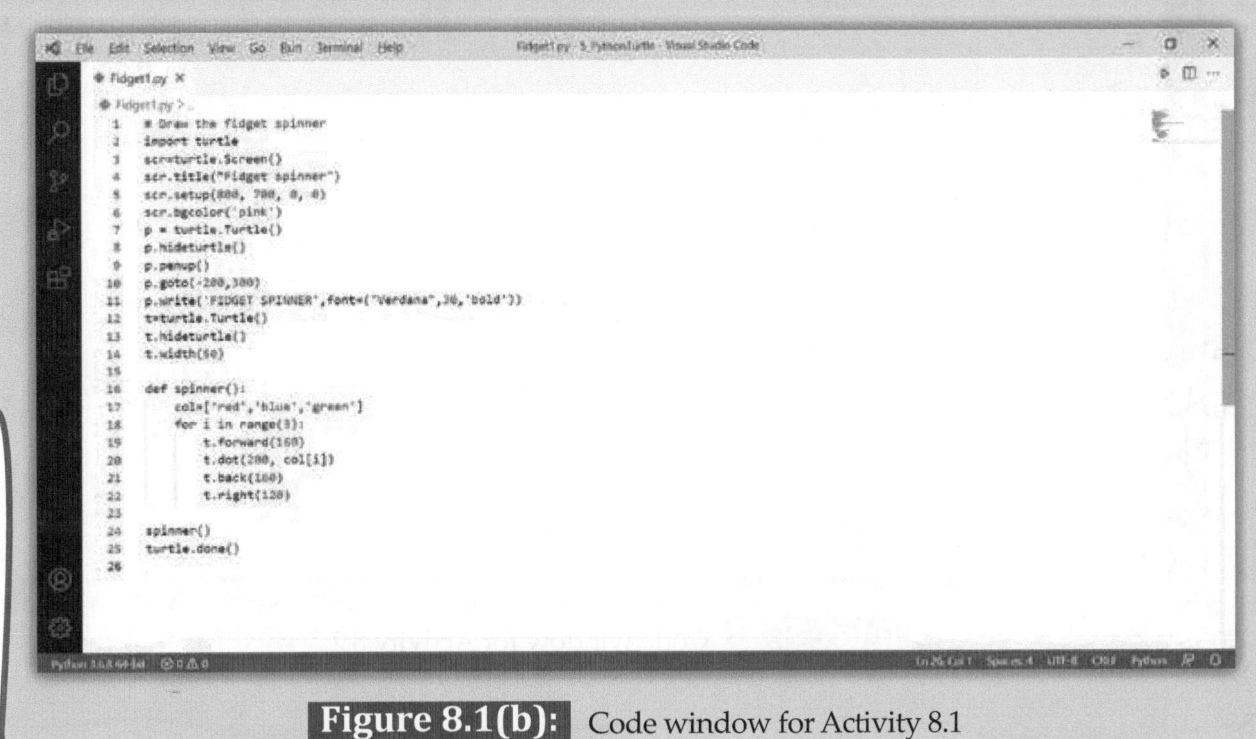

Figure 8.1(b): Code window for Activity 8.1

Activity 8.2

Write the functionality to the above activity so that the fidget starts spinning as soon as the user is going to click on Space bar key. The speed will increase if the user is going to keep clicking the Space bar key.

Declare the state for the spinner to be set in the beginning.

Create the user-defined function animate() to animate the fidget spinner. This function will keep checking the value of state, if it is greater than 0, it decreases its value by 1 and keep calling itself after every 10 milliseconds.

Create a user-defined function flick() that is invoked when the user clicks on space key to accelerate the fidget spinner by 20. Change the acceleration speed by changing this 20.

Add the following code as shown in figure 8.2 after the line number 15 in the above activity shown in the figure 8.1(b)

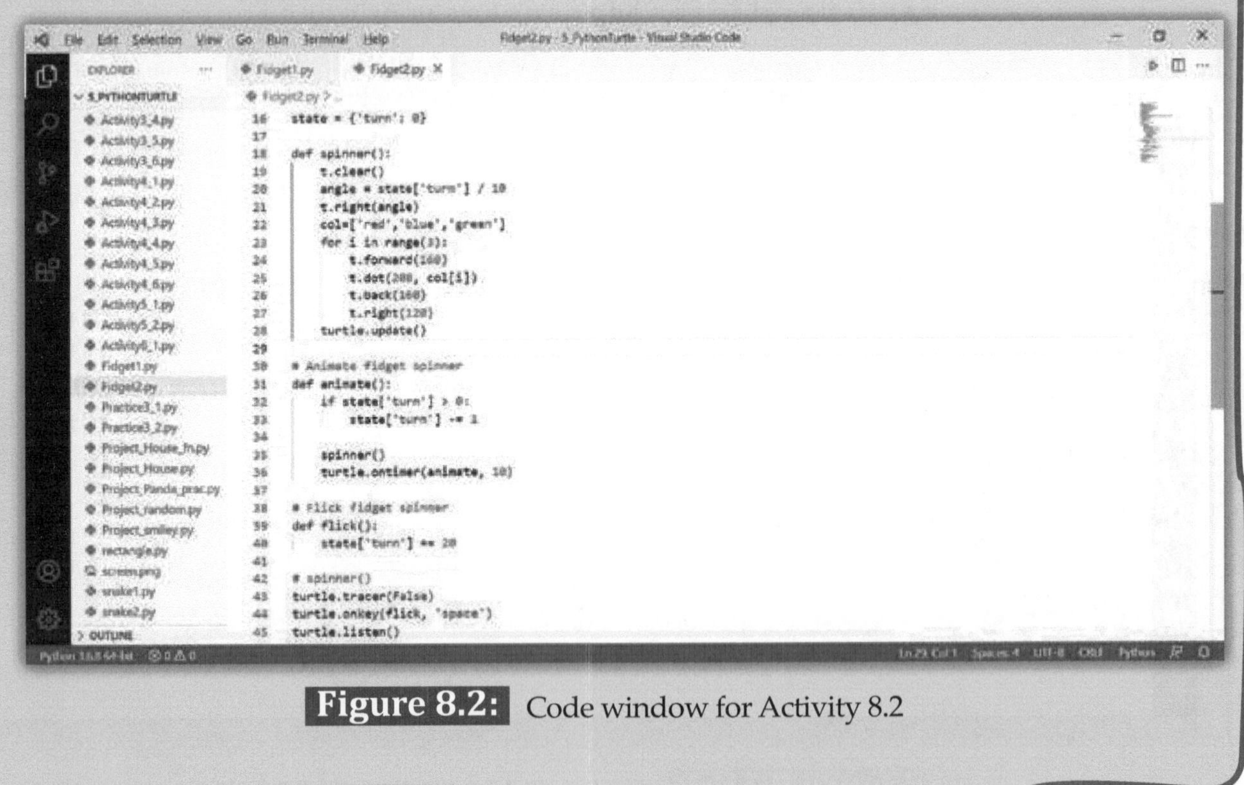

```
state = {'turn': 0}

def spinner():
    t.clear()
    angle = state['turn'] / 10
    t.right(angle)
    col=['red','blue','green']
    for i in range(3):
        t.forward(100)
        t.dot(200, col[i])
        t.back(100)
        t.right(120)
    turtle.update()

# Animate fidget spinner
def animate():
    if state['turn'] > 0:
        state['turn'] -= 1

    spinner()
    turtle.ontimer(animate, 10)

# Flick fidget spinner
def flick():
    state['turn'] += 20

# spinner()
turtle.tracer(False)
turtle.onkey(flick, 'space')
turtle.listen()
```

Figure 8.2: Code window for Activity 8.2

Info Bot

- Set tracer (False) to turn off the tracing while the turtle is moving. Need to use the update() function to keep updating the drawing. Tracer() and Update() functions are used for animation control.
- clear() function is used to delete the turtle drawings from the screen.
- onkey() function is a binder to the key-release event of the key. It registers the key-events on the turtle screen.
- ontimer() function is used to call the specified function after the given milliseconds.

Game – Snake

STRUCTURE

In this chapter, you will learn and practice the following concepts:

- Turtle module
- Time module
- Random module
- Concept of Python
- Event handling
- While loop
- Dictionary operation

LEARNING OBJEXCTIVE

At the end of this chapter, you will be able to:

- Initialise the state of the drawing object, angles for rotating it
- Animate the fidget spinner by checking the condition of its state
- Install the timer to call the user-defined function animate() again and again after a specific time in milliseconds

Activity 9.1

Create the game screen with the score board as title of the canvas having score and high score. Display the food and write the key binding functions for up, down, left and right directions.

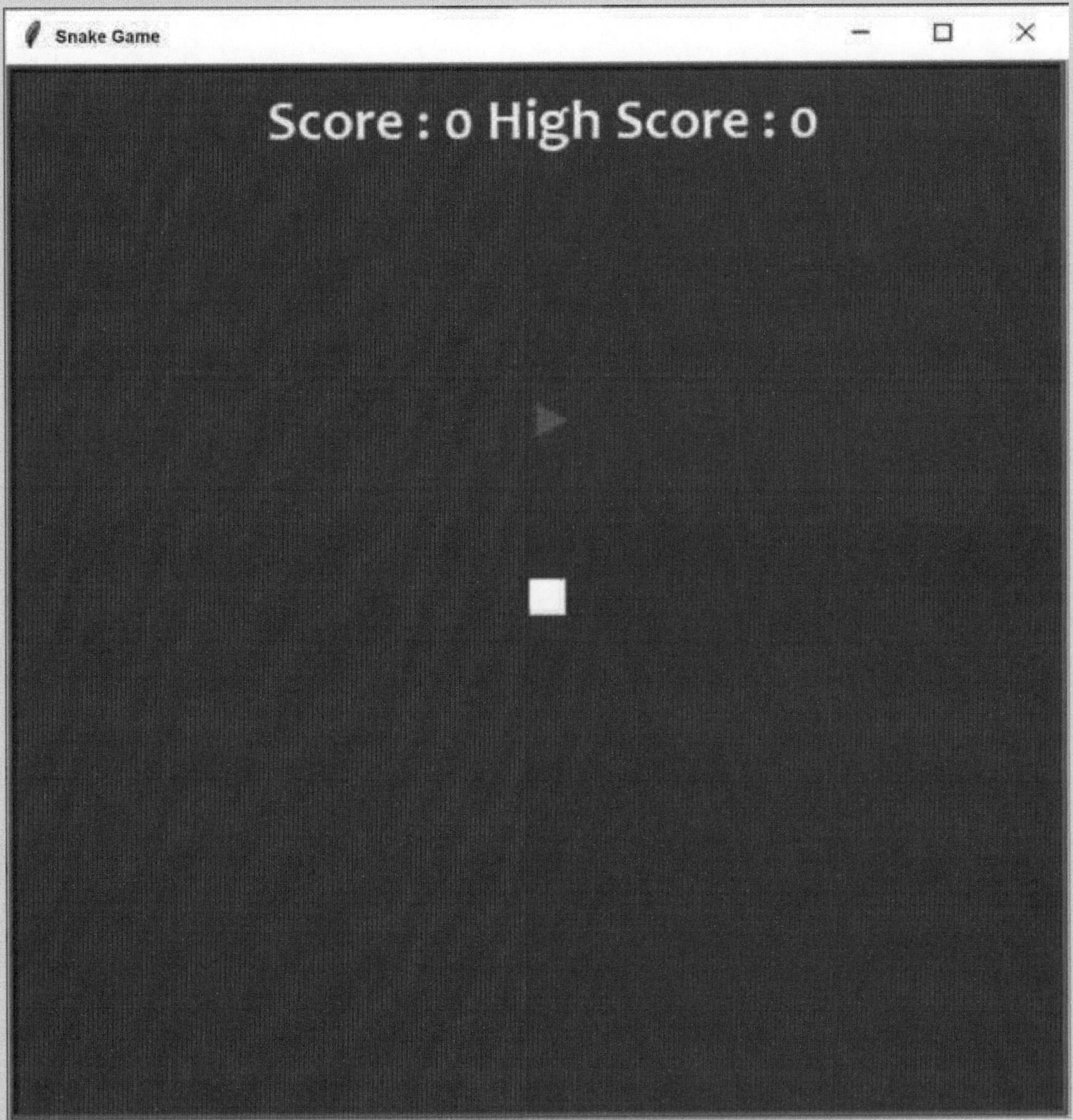

Snake Game

Score : 0 High Score : 0

Figure 9.1(a): Output window for Activity 9.1

```
# main loop
while True:
    win.update()
    if head.xcor()>290 or head.xcor()<-290 or head.ycor()>290 or head.ycor()<-290:
        time.sleep(1)
        head.goto(0, 0)
        head.direction = "Stop"

        for segment in segments:
            segment.goto(1000, 1000)
        segments.clear()
        score = 0
        delay = 0.1
        scrbrd.clear()
        scrbrd.write("Score : {} High Score : {} ".format(
            score, high_score), align="center", font=("candara", 24, "bold"))
    if head.distance(food) < 20:
        x = random.randint(-270, 270)
        y = random.randint(-270, 270)
        colors = random.choice(['red', 'blue', 'green'])
        shapes = random.choice(['triangle', 'circle'])
        food.shape(shapes)
        food.color(colors)
        food.goto(x, y)

        # Adding segment
        new_segment = turtle.Turtle()
        new_segment.speed(0)
        new_segment.shape("square")
        new_segment.color("orange")  # tail colour
        new_segment.penup()
        segments.append(new_segment)
        delay -= 0.001
        score += 10
        if score > high_score:
            high_score = score
        scrbrd.clear()
        scrbrd.write("Score : {} High Score : {} ".format(
            score, high_score), align="center", font=("candara", 24, "bold"))
```

```
 # Move the end segments first in reverse order
    for index in range(len(segments)-1, 0, -1):
        x = segments[index-1].xcor()
        y = segments[index-1].ycor()
        segments[index].goto(x, y)
    if len(segments) > 0:
        x = head.xcor()
        y = head.ycor()
        segments[0].goto(x, y)

# key directions
def up():
    if head.direction!='down':
        head.direction='up'

def down():
    if head.direction!='up':
        head.direction='down'

def left():
    if head.direction!='right':
        head.direction='left'

def right():
    if head.direction!='left':
        head.direction='right'

def move():
    if head.direction=='up':
        y=head.ycor()
        head.sety(y+20)
    if head.direction=='down':
        y=head.ycor()
        head.sety(y-20)
    if head.direction=='left':
        x=head.xcor()
        head.setx(x-20)
    if head.direction=='right':
```

```
        x=head.xcor()
        head.setx(x+20)

win.listen()
win.onkeypress(up,'w')
win.onkeypress(down,'x')
win.onkeypress(left,'a')
win.onkeypress(right,'d')

segments=[]
# main loop
while True:
    win.update()
    move()
    time.sleep(delay)

turtle.done()
```

Figure 9.1(b): Code window for Activity 9.1

Info Bot

screen.listen() function is used to keep checking for any key events taking place.

Activity 9.2

Write the functionality of snake collision with any of the borders (left, right, top, and bottom), functionality of snake collision with fruit to increase the score and generate food at random location, functionality of snake collision with its own body.

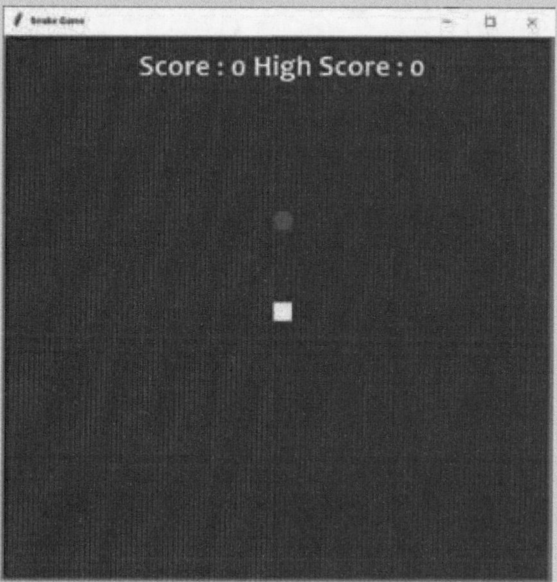

Figure 9.2(a): Output window for Activity

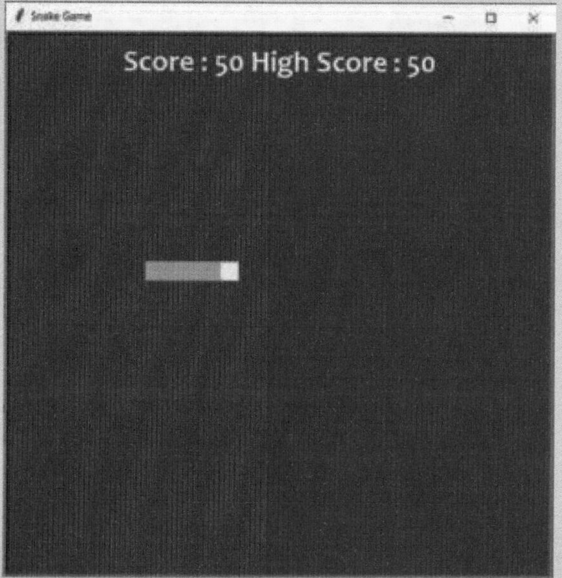

Figure 9.2(b): Output window for Activity 9.2

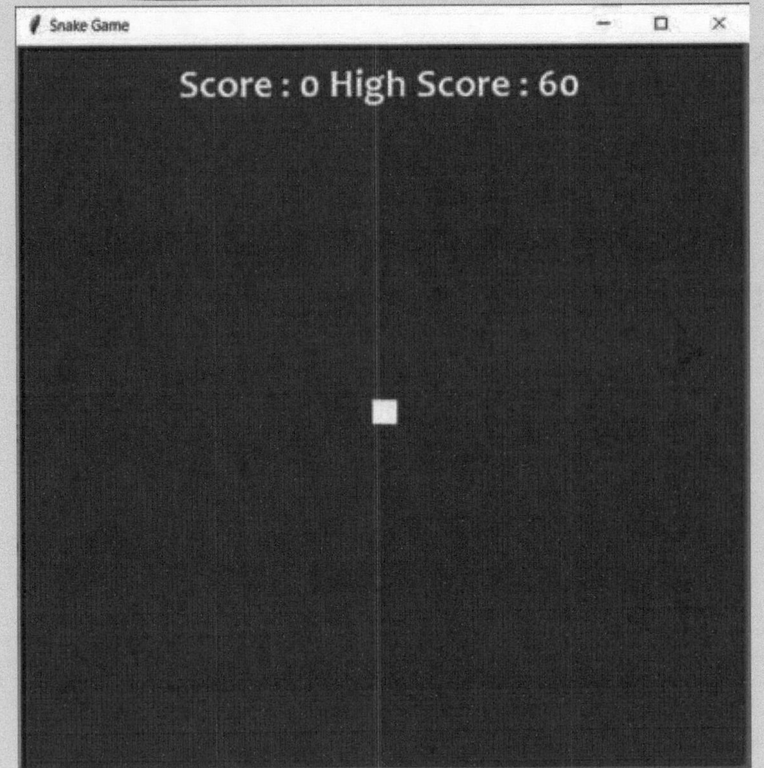

Figure 9.2(c): Output window for Activity 9.2

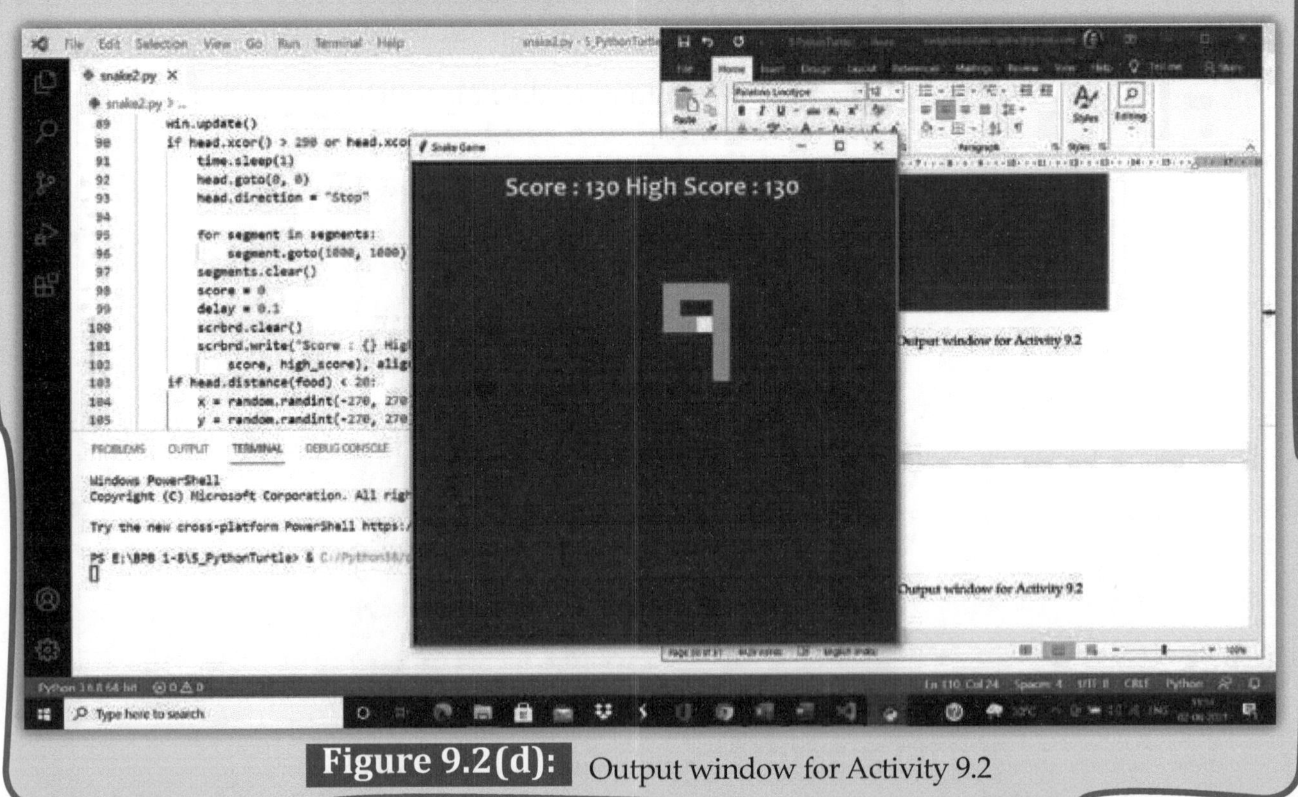

Figure 9.2(d): Output window for Activity 9.2

Now write the main logic of the game once again to play the game as is shown in the ***figures 9.1 (a), 9.1(b), 9.1(c), and 9.1(d).***

```
# main loop
while True:
    win.update()
    if head.xcor()>290 or head.xcor()<-290 or head.ycor()>290 or head.ycor()<-290:
        time.sleep(1)
        head.goto(0, 0)
        head.direction = "Stop"

        for segment in segments:
            segment.goto(1000, 1000)
        segments.clear()
        score = 0
        delay = 0.1
        scrbrd.clear()
        scrbrd.write("Score : {} High Score : {} ".format(
            score, high_score), align="center", font=("candara", 24, "bold"))
    if head.distance(food) < 20:
        x = random.randint(-270, 270)
        y = random.randint(-270, 270)
        colors = random.choice(['red', 'blue', 'green'])
        shapes = random.choice(['triangle', 'circle'])
        food.shape(shapes)
        food.color(colors)
        food.goto(x, y)

        # Adding segment
        new_segment = turtle.Turtle()
        new_segment.speed(0)
        new_segment.shape("square")
        new_segment.color("orange")  # tail colour
        new_segment.penup()
        segments.append(new_segment)
        delay -= 0.001
```

```
        score += 10
        if score > high_score:
            high_score = score
        scrbrd.clear()
        scrbrd.write("Score : {} High Score : {} ".format(
            score, high_score), align="center", font=("candara", 24, "bold"))

# Move the end segments first in reverse order
    for index in range(len(segments)-1, 0, -1):
        x = segments[index-1].xcor()
        y = segments[index-1].ycor()
        segments[index].goto(x, y)
    if len(segments) > 0:
        x = head.xcor()
        y = head.ycor()
        segments[0].goto(x, y)

    move()
    for segment in segments:
        if segment.distance(head) < 20:
            time.sleep(1)
            head.goto(0, 0)
            head.direction = "stop"

            for segment in segments:
                segment.goto(1000, 1000)
            segment.clear()

            score = 0
            delay = 0.1
            scrbrd.clear()
            scrbrd.write("Score : {} High Score : {} ".format(
                score, high_score), align="center", font=("candara", 24, "bold"))
    time.sleep(delay)

turtle.done()
```


Figure 9.2(e): Code window for Activity 9.2